The Common People Are Not Nothing

Plate 1 Arthur Capel, 1st Earl of Essex (1631-83) and his wife Elizabeth (1636-1718) by Sir Peter Lely, [National Portrait Gallery].

The Common People Are Not Nothing:

Conflict in Religion and Politics in Hertfordshire 1575-1780

Lionel M Munby

HERTFORDSHIRE PUBLICATIONS
1995

HERTFORDSHIRE PUBLICATIONS
(Hertfordshire Libraries, Arts & Information, in association with Hertfordshire Association for Local History).

New Barnfield, Travellers Lane,
Hatfield, Hertfordshire, AL10 8XG

ISBN 0-901354-80-5

Printed by the Broadwater Press Ltd., Welwyn Garden City

I dedicate this book to all those people who, over many years, have joined me in studying Hertfordshire history in adult education classes.

L.M.M.

CONTENTS

LIST OF PLATES

LIST OF MAPS, FIGURES & TABLES

ABBREVIATIONS

BL. Add Ms.	British Library Additional Manuscript
DNB.	*Dictionary of National Biography*
HCRO.	Hertfordshire County Record Office
HMC.	Historical Manuscripts Commission
OED.	*Oxford English Dictionary*
VCH.	*Victoria County History*

PREFACE

The seven distinct studies of aspects of Hertfordshire history brought together in this book have more in common than may appear at first sight. In one way or another they all reveal the reverse side of traditional history. Common to all the studies is an inversion, a turning upside down of what has been a conventional view point. Certain themes connect distinct chapters: the existence of a continuing undercurrent of social opposition to the established society from Tudor times into the eighteenth century; the ways in which this found religious forms of expression; the linkage which developed between religious and political opposition to the dominant order. The history of the period involved, the century following the restoration of Charles II in 1660, can only be understood if it is looked at from below as well as from above. From time to time these local studies impinge on national history; it is hoped that they may be of interest to many people who do not have any special interest in Hertfordshire's history, as well as to those who do.

The first chapter, which covers an earlier period than the century within which the other six fall, is a necessary introduction, to provide an historical perspective to the chapter which follows. Unless the long term existence of a discontented, anti-authoritarian section of society is appreciated, the emergence of widespread public hostility to the establishment during the 1640s and 1650s cannot be understood; nor can the survival and revival of hostility between 1660 and the 1680s. Religious and political dissent became intertwined, religion and 'party' politics were connected. This is the theme followed through in the later studies. The melodrama of the so-called Rye House 'plot' and supposed suicide of the Earl of Essex is parallelled by the trial of a future judge for the supposed murder of a Quaker girl. In chapter 3 the extreme form taken by the tensions and violent conflicts which led to the so-called Glorious Revolution of 1688 is revealed. In the following chapters the diminution of such violence, by the end of the seventeenth century and in the eighteenth century, appears; but conflict continues in bitter party politics. The history of two families, Caesars and Dimsdales, links these last four chapters. The fall of the Jacobite Caesars contrasts with the rise of the Quaker Dimsdales, who followed the profession of medicine through five generations. The Society of Friends features in Chapter 2 and in the last four chapters.

The events and the themes covered in this book have interested me for many years and, I believe, each story is of interest in itself and that each study could stand on its own. However I have come to realise that a closer look at even the most apparently distinct topics reveals interesting and unexpected links between them. It was the appreciation of the loose connecting threads joining the stories which persuaded me to bring them together into a book.

Everything in this book owes its existence to the stimulus I have received over decades from the very many Hertfordshire people who have come to the adult classes which I have taken for the University of Cambridge Board of Extra-Mural Studies and the Workers Educational Association. The debt I owe them is not merely because they have flattered my ego by listening to me but, more importantly, because they have stretched my mind and stimulated my curiosity by intelligent questioning and criticism. It is to them that I dedicate this book in gratitude.

I could not have written Chapters 5 and 6 without the access which the late Tom Cottrell Dormer of Rousham gave me to the Caesar papers which his family possess. I was not only given access but treated with much courtesy. Chapter 7 has been much improved thanks to the assistance which Robert Dimsdale of Barkway has given me, in particular with the American references. The staff of the County Record Office and of the Local Studies Collection at Hertford have, as always, been most helpful, whenever I have wanted any information. Permission to reproduce photographs from the British Library, British Museum, Hertfordshire County Record Office, the National Portrait Gallery and Trinity College, Cambridge, is gratefully acknowledged. My thanks are due to Sandra Bicknell for drawing the two maps, to Graham Javes my editor at Hertfordshire Publications, for his meticulous concern for precision, and finally to Diana my wife, who has not only transformed my impossible handwriting into type-script but is responsible for the index of people and places.

Lionel M Munby
Cambridge 1995

PART ONE

THE COMMON PEOPLE OF HERTFORDSHIRE REBEL
1575-1683/8

~ 1 ~
THE COMMON PEOPLE ARE NOT NOTHING
1575-1625

That great American poet, Walt Whitman, wrote in 1855 in his
To Think of Time:

> The interminable hordes of the ignorant and wicked are not nothing,
> The barbarians of Africa and Asia are not nothing,
> The common people of Europe are not nothing – the American
> aborigines are not nothing,
> The infected in the immigrant hospital are not nothing – the mur-
> derer or mean person is not nothing,
> The perpetual succession of shallow people are not nothing as
> they go,
> The lowest prostitute is not nothing – the mocker of religion is not
> nothing as he goes.[1]

The historian, who 'thinks of Time' as Whitman does, faces difficulties. The hordes of the ignorant and wicked, the shallow people,
murderers and mean people, prostitutes and mockers of religion –
these kinds of common people – were far from nothing in Elizabethan
and Stuart England, *but* they left no individual, personal records.
They were only documented when the law caught up with them.

Contemporaries despised, feared and punished the unsuccessful,
the social outcasts, the nonconformists, as do all societies. William
Harrison wrote of 'three sorts' of poor in his *Description of England* in
the 1570s: 'some are poor by impotence . . . the second are poor by
casualty . . . the third consisteth of the thriftless poor . . . For the first
two sorts (. . . which are the true poor indeed, and for whom the Word
doth bind us to make some daily provision), there is order taken
throughout every parish in the realm that weekly collection shall be
made for their help . . . the third sort . . ., instead of courteous refresh-
ing at home, are often corrected with sharp execution and whip of justice abroad.'[2] The Elizabethan Poor Laws of 1598 and 1601 made a parallel distinction between the 'number of good and able subjects [in
whom] a good part of the strength of this realm consisteth' and the
'great number of poor people [who] are become wanderers, idle and
loose.'[3] Parish rates were to be levied to care for the first group when
in need, the law was to deal firmly and harshly with the second cate-
gory of poor. The respectable poor are documented in parish records
and their story has been told in innumerable local histories. The outcasts appear rarely in parish records; their story can only be pieced
together from lawcourt records, on which this study is almost entirely
based.[4] However such records tell only one side of the story: they are

not necessarily untrue but, at the best, 'economical with the truth'!

This study is concerned, firstly, with the 'thriftless poor', 'wanderers, idle and loose' in late Elizabethan and early Stuart Hertfordshire, who they were, why they became vagrants and how women were most at risk. Vagrants were often identified with thieves and murderers though these criminals most often, in practice, were members of settled communities. What the two groups did share was the alehouse. The second group of common people with whom this study is concerned are the 'lewd and unchristian young men' and women who attacked persons and property, physically, and defamed the church and government in words. It ends with those people, women for the most part, who were accused of practising witchcraft.

'Wanderers, idle and loose' – vagrants

In any Hertfordshire parish near to a through road, and in many others, the parish registers will contain entries like those from Hunsdon. Hunsdon, in the sixteenth century, was on the main Norwich – Newmarket – London road. So it is not surprising that 'Dennys Clapham, the son of a walkinge man' was christened on 13 October 1559 and buried on 11 November 1560. 'An old man which came out of the north died in Cuthbert Chambers' house' and was buried on 15 February 1584; and 'Goodman Mathew, a bucher by trade and a stranger, borne about Colchester' was buried on 24 September 1599. 'Thomas Cocke sonne of Thomas Cock a poor wanderer whose wiffe brought furth a child at Hunsdon Mill' was christened on 1 February 1607.[5] The settled members of the local community suspected the wanderer, the vagrant, of being a thief or purveyor of stolen goods or, even worse, of being seditious. Richard Fettle of Westmill, a labourer, was described in 1589 as an idle and vagrant fellow' who did not work but 'liveth very suspiciously'. This type of descriptive comment appears frequently in the records. Another labourer, Edward Smyth of Sawbridgeworth, was described in 1590 as a vagrant soldier who had failed to return to his place of settlement.

There are contemporary descriptions of vagabonds from which lists of the different categories as seen at the time can be compiled. They are revealing and, incidentally, amusing. There were 'masterless' men, who refused to work, 'and who hoped by threats or begging' to make a living. There were 'disbanded soldiers, who . . . refused to abandon the freedom of idleness'. There were 'bands of adventurers, whose trades made vagabondage inevitable: . . . fencers; . . . ballad-mongers and minstrels who carried sedition up and down the country in their songs; bearwards . . .; common players; . . . "bawkers" who haunted bowling-alleys to cozen the poor fools who resorted thither for sport; scholars of Oxford and Cambridge who went abroad begging without the authority of the Vice-Chancellor; shipmen pretending losses at sea;

together with a vast mob of jugglers, tinkers, and petty chapmen.'[6]

What the national government thought of vagrants was put bluntly by John Williams, Bishop of Lincoln and Lord Keeper of the Great Seal, who wrote officially to the Hertfordshire JPs on 21 September 1622, informing them that 'the common and statute laws of this kingdom... do utterly condemn and extirpate beggars, rogues, vagabonds, Egyptians [gipsies], and such lazy and unprofitable members of the commonwealth'. The JPs had allowed the county 'to swarm with whole troups of [such] idle persons'. They must enforce the 'laws for the punishing, employing, chastising and rooting out of these idle people (symptoms of Popery and blind superstition)', a revealing indication that the government identified vagrancy with sedition, for that is what Roman Catholicism was thought to be. The economic aspect of vagrancy was appreciated, for the same letter ordered the JPs to curb 'excessive and intolerable prices' of foodstuffs. 'You shall enjoin your constables to present at every Quarter Sessions all those former troupings of rogues and vagabonds and all excessive prices'.

In fact the local constables had been pursuing and punishing vagrants for years. Any stranger was liable to be whipped, sent to the county's House of Correction, and then moved on to the parish in which he was thought to have a legal settlement under the Poor Law. In 1596-7 local alehouse keepers were ordered by the JPs only to accommodate people they could answer for. They were to report to the constables the names, the dwelling place if known, and the clothing of anyone who stayed two days before or two days after any robbery. Nothing was to be bought from a wayfarer without the constable being told, in case the goods had been stolen. The implied assumption that vagrancy and theft went hand in hand is not born out by the court records. Vagrants in Hertfordshire were rarely prosecuted for any other offences than begging or being a stranger without obvious means of support. In one of the few cases where vagrants were connected with a crime, their existence may have been invented by the defendant to mitigate her offence. Two Hitchin spinsters confessed that they had used Alice Gould, perhaps a young girl, to 'collect' goods stolen in two thefts in Great Wymondley in August 1593. Alice's defence in a third theft was that she had been persuaded by two strange vagabond women to look through Edward Bygrave's window. They put her through the window to collect the russet gown and black felt hat she saw, took the clothes and left her; not a very likely story perhaps.

There were fairly simple reasons why the authorities failed completely to 'extirpate beggars, rogues, vagabonds, Egyptians'. When we read that the keeper of the Hertford House of Correction, Oliver Holland, was accused in 1622 of harbouring William Pecke, 'a common rogue coming to him with stolen goods', we begin to wonder whether the keeper was a receiver, hardly the man to set vagrants on the straight and narrow path. The high constable of Odsey Hundred certified to Assizes in July 1609 that he had ordered the constables of every parish in his division to 'watch one day in a week and make privy search one night in a week for the apprehension of such' vagrants, but only four parishes made returns. The laxity of parish constables, who were ordinary villagers pressed into service for a year at a time, was understandable. It could be dangerous to be too officious: vagrants had friends. In 1613 William Nottage of Braughing rescued an idle rogue from the custody of the Standon constable. The fate of John Trott, constable of Redbourn in 1623, was a warning. He was 'called out of his bed in the dead-time of night by certain strangers that passed through the town'. He found a great company fighting in the street, called for aid, and tried to part them. He was wounded ten times and lost the use of some of his limbs. He had spent all he had 'in seeking the cure', but Quarter Sessions, when applied to for a life pension, merely granted him £1 down and another £1 the next year, after which the records are silent. There was only one sure way of getting rid of the unwanted, as the constable of Codicote reported in July 1609, 'insomuch that it pleased god to visit us with the pestilence, all the vagrant persons refrained the town'.

Most vagrants had been squeezed out or were thrown out by the settled members of an ordered society. Whatever they became they began not as criminals but as people others could put upon because they were poor. Communities with few reserves could not easily afford to keep anyone unemployed or unemployable, or families without a wage earner. The inhabitants of Aston complained in 1596 that sixty-year-old Margaret Field was a charge on the parish. She was lame and not able to work: Thomas Betts, for whom she had worked for twenty-two years for no wages, refused to support her. He had swindled her: ten or twelve years earlier she had handed him a legacy in return for his promise to keep her for the rest of her life in drink, lodging and clothing. At Michaelmas of the same year, 1596, Simon Howe, an Ardeley labourer, abandoned his wife and children with only an unheated shed to live in. The family became a charge on the inhabitants. When the cold weather came Thomas Shotbolt, the local JP, persuaded Philip Cooke to let them live in his hay-house and make a fireplace there. By midsummer 1597 Cooke wanted the house back to store hay and corn, but agreed to leave Howe's family until Michaelmas. However he was afraid the lord of the manor would take advantage of him for maintaining them. Howe was a thoroughly bad character. He brought a young child into his old house which the inhabitants feared might become a further charge on the local rates. He did not work, which led Shotbolt to presume he was living by unlawful means. To cap it all he had not been to church between Michaelmas 1596 and Michaelmas 1597 and had been excommunicated!

We do not know what happened to Margaret Field or to Simon Howe's wife and children, but these were the kinds of people who were rejected by their communities and became wanderers. Many of the men who became vagrants, fleeing from poverty and from their responsibilities, may have had rather more choice than the women. There must have been many characters like John Bascombe, a chapman who, in 1601, sold small wares at Bishops Stortford; he had left his lawful wife, kept another woman as wife and had no habitation or dwelling place. There were more unusual wanderers: the most remarkable to appear before Hertfordshire Quarter Sessions was Thomas Arnold, physician and surgeon, who was examined by the JPs in 1589-90 and explained himself as follows: 'he hath travelled into France, Italy, and Germany, and was there when the old Earl of Arundel was at Padua; . . . he taught Mr Walter Hastings, Mr John Sellenger, Mr Robert Dormer, and Mr George Shelley . . . by the space of four months . . . ; he dwelled eight years . . . within six miles of Monmouth, and his wife died four years past with two of her children of the plague . . . ; he came from thence about three quarters of a year past, whereof half a year he hath dwelled at Cheshunt . . . ; he went from Cheshunt to Ware, and there altered his name because he would not have the woman which he got with child there to follow him, . . . his meaning was, after he got some money in his purse, to have gone into the country where he was born and to have returned back again unto her and to have married her.'

Women at risk

Women, particularly servants, were most vulnerable. A sexual adventurer, the butcher Leonard Beeker employed by Robert Wood of Hertford, seduced an honest girl, Margaret Springham, Wood's servant. This happened a week before Margaret left Wood's service. In 1594 Beeker admitted that he had promised to marry Margaret Springham but after she left had fathered a child on another Margaret whom he betrothed but also abandoned. He ran off with a third woman whom he actually married, leaving no money for the maintenance of the two servant girls or the bastard child. He crowned his 'most vile and vicious life' with theft and swindling. Peter Coxe of Thundridge behaved in a similar way. In 1590 he fathered a child on Isabel Goodrich and was carted through Thundridge 'barefaced' with her. Three years later he repeated his offence with an Isabell Dickenson from Enfield. Her employers, the Enfield curate, and a widow gave evidence that Coxe had tried to bribe and threaten Isabell and her employers to make them say that they had been paid to claim Coxe was the father of Isabell's child.

If the parish could not find a father to pay for the infant, the wretched woman might end up like Alice Usher, a single woman of

Cheshunt, who was found wandering in the countryside in 1620 with her child. It is no accident that the spinster seems to have been the most persecuted woman in the Elizabethan and early Stuart community. Spinsters were punished for producing illegitimate children, accused of infanticide if the children died, and suspected of witchcraft. Spinsters and widows were particularly vulnerable if they became pregnant. Twelve cases of rape came before the courts; the age of the woman was given in six of them and three were girls not yet in their teens. The local community might reject the miserable mother. She would be ruthlessly cross-examined while in childbirth. On the night of 19 September 1590 Julian Heath fell into labour; she was asked who was the father. The midwife and eight other women heard her answer her late master's brother, who had told her he would give her a powder to drink to get rid of the child, which 'she would not, for . . . as she had offended for the begetting she would not offend double in the destruction thereof'.

We have detailed 'articles' revealing how one local lecher, Thomas Kent of Aston, prayed upon women and persecuted them for informing on him. He used threats, force and bribes, apparently without success. He told his own maid servant, Mary Bullerd, that because she was his servant she had no right to make public his behaviour to her. He carried another servant, Joan Wyberd, into a loft at Bragbury End in Datchworth by force; she was saved because a woman heard her cries and burst open the door. Two married women were offered bribes. Kent thrust his hands between the legs of John Cowper's wife and then offered her a bushel of apples for the carnal use of her body as the court jargon put it. John Cooke's wife, Elizabeth, was pulled into Kent's house when she went to fetch a gimlet he had borrowed. He tried to seduce her, offering her a bushel of wheat and 'thrusting money into her bosom'. She told him that he had a 'proper fair woman' as wife, while she was 'but a black wench'. When Kent said one woman was not enough for him, he needed black wenches in corners, Elizabeth told him to go to those of that disposition, but he replied every man and woman was. 'Weary with striving and wrestling to get out of his lecherous company', she promised to let him have his way some other time. Kent remembered and one day when she was gathering 'kypes', probably osiers, he ran after her, saying 'Come, come, tybb, let me occupy thee, for thou didst promise me'. She frightened Kent off by shouting as loud as she could. Tybb was a familiar word for a girl, a sweetheart, with the implication of lower class or even of loose character.

Joan Reve of Baldock had given evidence against Kent and he revenged himself for her 'evil will', presenting her for leaving church and citing her and six other women to appear before the Archdeacon's Court at Huntingdon. They were too poor and the 'care and charge' of their children was too great for them to travel so far; so they were excommunicated for not appearing. Kent 'in scoffing manner' had told them that no JP would take any matter of his in hand unless he chose. There is an interesting footnote to the story. On 1 May 1590 Thomas Betts of Aston, who six years later was said to have refused to support his sixty-year-old servant, was attacked by Kent in the chancel of Hitchin church. Kent struck Betts with his staff and drew blood: he was prosecuted under a statute which laid down as penalty branding in the cheek or losing an ear. Kent's quarrel with Betts was because it was Betts who had reported Kent's attack on the maid in the loft; Kent also blamed Betts for the Baldock women's complaints. Was Kent behind the complaint about Betts' neglect of his old servant made by Aston inhabitants six years later, in 1596?

A series of events which took place in Pirton, in 1589, one year earlier than the Kent affair, shows how accusations of sexual behaviour were used in spite. The intricate tale was told by Thomas Auncell. A Mr Copcot and William Hammond had taken Thomas' brother, Robert, before the Star Chamber Court at great expense because Robert had thrown down some new enclosures of theirs. 'Not having their minds of him as they thought they should', Copcot and Hammond looked for revenge. A certain Cranfield from Shefford was persuaded to try to make Robert's wife jealous by implicating him with Alice. Hanscome. Some poor men were induced to sign Cranfield's libel; they later admitted they had not read it. When Robert's wife refused to accuse Alice Hanscome of being an errant whore, she was kept at Mr Copcot's house against her husband's will. Meanwhile one of the churchwardens was persuaded to present Robert, presumably to a church court, for adultery. Since the other churchwarden and the sidesmen, who were Robert's brothers, did not join in the accusation, the court considered it void. Thomas Auncell blamed Mr Copcot's wife for the false accusation against his brother Robert. Like many of the pinhole peepshows which court records afford, there are curious loose ends to the story. Why did Robert's brothers agree, as churchwardens and sidesmen, to present Robert's wife 'of a common fame of unchaste life'? Who hung what libels against the minister and other Pirton inhabitants on the maypole and broadcast them in Hitchin? Weapons were drawn; by whom and why?

Thieves and murderers

What kept the lawcourts busiest was theft. There were literally hundreds of cases of grand and petty larceny, fewer of burglary and highway robbery. The objects stolen are interesting. How far they provide clues to social needs or to human greed as opposed to revealing which objects could be most easily stolen must be a matter of speculation. Only 81 cases of food being stolen came before Assizes between 1575 and 1625, but there were 827 cases of stolen cloth and clothes. As many as 20 of the 53 cases of stolen food in Queen Elizabeth's reign were of spices, cloves, ginger, mace, nutmeg, pepper, raisins and sugar. The most frequently stolen items of clothing were: shirts and shirt bands (91), hose and stockings (78), kerchiefs and rails (72) both of which were cloths worn round women's necks, hats and caps (71). There were 37 cases of aprons being stolen, 36 of smocks and only 27 of boots or shoes. Animals were stolen in well over 500 cases but grain only in under 100. There were 100 cases of purses or wallets being stolen and 224 thefts of money. Overwhelmingly it was labourers who were prosecuted for simple theft, that is grand or petty larceny, while yeomen and craftsmen bulk larger among those accused of the less common burglary and high-way robbery. All these offences were largely male crimes; only a few women were accused of them. Gentlemen, yeomen, and women when accused of these crimes were much more likely to be found not guilty, or to be punished lightly when guilty, than labourers or craftsmen.

Sometimes robbery and burglary led to murder. On 11 September 1587 Laurence Danbye, a Cheshunt butcher, was robbed of £100; his neck was broken and his body thrown into the river. On 14 December 1600 Margaret Eldredge, the servant of John Seare of Puttenham, was killed by a burglar who hit her with the fire shovel. Fights were respon-sible for sixteen of the thirty cases of homicide which came before Assizes between 1576 and 1624. Where the attacker died the court accepted a plea of self-defence. Some murders seem to have been senseless and unprovoked: in 1576 two men, a painter and a shoe-maker from Aylesbury, went looking for a fight in Kings Langley; they killed two men in separate attacks. There is only one case of suicide listed in the period covered by these court records. 'One Robert Stapeleton of Wormley, cheese (or scythe?) maker' was presented to Quarter Sessions in 1591 'for hanging of himself'.

Deliberate murder, murder which was not a by-product of robbery or fighting, was a crime of which women were often accused, though only one woman was found guilty and hung. Two married women were acquitted of being accessories before the fact in a peculiarly revolting murder in Berkhamsted in 1597. John Winchester, a yeoman, was hung for killing John Bristoe, a local gentleman, by forcing a sheathed knife down his throat. Bristoe's wife was one of the two women who were acquitted. There were three cases in which women were supposed to have put ratsbane (arsenic) in stews, curds, porridge or a posset; but in only one case was the woman found guilty and hung. Altogether thirteen people, three of whom confessed, one being this woman, were hung for murder; four more guilty men were allowed clergy; and three were found guilty of homicide, not murder. Eleven of the thirty-nine accused, six of the seven women, were found not guilty. In another eight cases the court did not reach a verdict. It was a different matter in the fifteen accusations of infanticide in which nineteen people were involved. Perhaps it is not surprising that fourteen were spinsters, two wives, and two widows. Four of the spinsters and the only man accused were found guilty and hung. One widow confessed and was hung; she was Barbara Foster of Hunsdon. Her child, born on 28 February 1600, had been immediately put into an earthen pot and thrown into a pond. Other children had been kicked to death, beaten to death with a rolling pin, suffocated, strangled, squashed and thrown into a well, a stream, and the 'vault of an house of office', the lavatory.

Where there had clearly been a violent death and the accused was responsible but the court believed they were blameless, various legal fictions were employed. One murder was due to divine visitation; still birth was the explanation in some infanticide cases, probably quite reasonably in some if not all of them. Two verdicts, however, are especially interesting. In a murder case, the accused in self-defence had run his attacker through the chest with a rapier, but the court found that John Noke had killed the dead man, though no one else was present. The Elizabethan equivalent of a cot death was blamed on 'one at Noke' having suffocated the infant, though no one but the mother was present. Fictional personalities were a common device in legal disputes over titles to property; John Doe and Richard Roe were familiar invisible figures in court. John, or 'one at', Noke must have been a similar invisible participant in homicide cases.

Alehouses

Though thieves were not described as vagrants nor vagrants as thieves, they shared one common refuge. Their main place of comfort, their bolt holes, were the 'secret victualling houses, not licenced' against which the county's JPs fought a continuous and unsuccessful battle. Prosecutions of alehouse keepers continued throughout the late Tudor and early Stuart period. In March 1624 Assizes were informed that there were more than 540 alehouses in the county which the Grand Jury believed were 'nurseries of all vice and wickedness'. So much for two generations of activity by the authorities. We have several revealing descriptions of what alehouses could be like. A report was made to Quarter Sessions on four Hemel Hempstead alehouses or inns in December 1593. The local officials who made the report went to Richard Turner's where they found a weaver who did not work, a very 'lewd disposed fellow' who preferred the company of 'light women'; his wife insulted the bailiff when she was advised to 'amend his ways'. The other three houses visited were gambling dens. Richard Pope, though he had been prosecuted four years before and frequently admonished, was still allowing card games on his property:

a great gamester from Kings Langley who enticed young men was found in Pope's inn. William Coveney, the third innkeeper, used 'very taunting words' to a Mr Shad, one of the local inhabitants accompanying the bailiff on his inspection. Mr Shad received more 'very ill words' from a common gamester in the fourth house visited, Thomas Dyche's. One of the gamesters said he would play all night and if the constable or anyone else came he would knock 'their heads and the post together'. For a parting shot Dyche said the bailiff was as welcome as a dog; his guests hollered and threw water after the departing inspectors. True most of those mentioned were later arrested and punished, but whether this had any permanent effect is doubtful.

Many of the unwanted alehouses seem to have been near market towns and thoroughfares, by road junctions but a little out of the way. Hitchin and Ware appear often in the records but the most frequently mentioned place was Cheshunt. Cheshunt was allowed fourteen alehouses as against Hertford's twelve and Hoddesdon's eight at the 1596-7 licensing session for Hertford Hundred. The new marshal appointed in 1622 was told to concentrate on excluding rogues from the outborders, particularly Theobalds and Cheshunt where the king mostly resided. Twelve unlicensed Cheshunt alehouses were prosecuted in 1622. The king's presence may have stimulated the authorities into action but it was the main road out of London which brought the customers to the alehouses. As late as 1835 Hoddesdon was complaining about 'vagrancy . . . robberies and incendiary fires [on] the direct road from London to . . . the north'.

It is no accident that Robert Trimmer of Turnford, described in 1603-4 as 'an endship' of Cheshunt, was a common lodger 'of all baggage people, as rogues, tinkers, peddlars, and such like and cares not whom he receives, his house standing at the town's end, nor from whence they come, so he makes gain of them'. He was 'infected with an unwholesome disease' as his speech, hands and other parts of his body suggested. His wife was a notorious slut, 'not fit to keep a victualling', while his wife's daughter who lived with them was described as a 'common naughty-pack' with one bastard child and another on the way. Six years earlier John Stanfield of the Green Cloak in Layston, a few miles to the north, had been banned from keeping alehouses because his was 'a house of great disorders as well in entertaining of the worst sort of people as also by suffering swearing, gaming, drunkenness, quarrelling, and great suspicion of whoredom'.

The regular use of the phrase 'disordered persons' in describing the unwanted visitors to alehouses reflects the fear that if 'degree' was challenged the fabric of society would be threatened. Shakespeare expressed this Tudor fear in a famous speech by Ulysses in *Troilus and Cressida:*

'Take but degree away, untune that string,
And hark what discord follows! each thing meets
In mere oppugnancy'.

Ulysses goes on to argue that if
'The general's disdained
By him one step below; he, by the next',

and so on, everyone will become 'sick of his superior'. In 1623 ale-house keepers in Ware, Hertford and Hoddesdon were prosecuted for harbouring common rogues, 'disordered and suspected persons at unseasonable times', and servants at unlawful times without the 'priv-ity and against the consent of their masters'. In 1589 the unlicensed alehouse kept by William Hale of Little Gaddesden had been sup-pressed: for six years he had been 'keeping of men's servants when they should have been about their Masters' affairs, and [especially] in the night time'. Disobedient servants might easily join the ranks of wanderers.

There is a good deal of evidence that respect for 'order' and 'degree' was far from universal: when alehouses were closed there were always local people willing to shelter strangers, like widow Patmer of Eastwick who, in 1624, harboured an all night tippler, described as an unknown person of evil conversation which then meant a bad char-acter. A Hertingfordbury yeoman, Thomas Grubb, gave 'denocta-cionem', presumably overnight accommodation, to a vagabond, Robert Hewes. We get a rare but revealing picture of a locally organ-ised network of refuges for vagrants in 1636-41; there had probably been similar organisations earlier. Richard Haynes of Much Hadham was bound over as 'a common harbourer of rogues' in 1636. By 1641 he and his wife Susan were catering for as many as sixty, and seldom less than twenty, vagrants in their private house and barn where the couple allowed the vagrants' 'victuals to be usually dressed and their clothes to be frequently washed'. When the Much Hadham constables raided the Haynes' house, the vagrants took refuge in neighbouring parishes; a barn in Widford and another in Sawbridgeworth, belonging to widow Ward of Warrens, were mentioned. Since parish constables had no powers outside their own parish the county's JPs were asked to act so that 'the knot and concourse . . . may be broken' and the county freed from terrors; and this is how we come to hear about this underground union. A knot was a company of persons gathered together in one place, according to the *Oxford English Dictionary*.

Hoddesdon in 1590 and Cheshunt in 1598 experienced scenes of boozy disorder in which crowds got out of hand. 'The honest men of the town', the local constables, and even the local JP, Sir Henry Cock, were treated with contemptuous disrespect. On 16 September 1590 the Hoddesdon constable arrested two very poor men who played continually at cards 'to the great impoverishing of their wives and children'; one of them, 'often times over taken with drink, will beat his wife to the great disquiet of his honest neighbours'. Sir Henry Cock put him in the Cage, the parish lock-up, for gaming and 'abusing his tongue' and as an example to others. The second man brought drink to the Cage and there was 'great carousing . . . very likely . . . to make a mutiny'. The constables went to bring the second offender to the Cage but forgot to lock it. The 'bringing of pots and carousing' began again and William Tooke of Stanstead dragged the first man out of the Cage. On their way back the constables reproved a tapster with a pot and glass in his hand, but a bystander swore that 'he would see who durst say anything to him for giving drink in the Cage'. Joined by another man they returned to the Cage with their pots of beer which 'in very contemptuous manner [they] did drink', and one of them said he would spit in the constables' faces.

St Giles' Fair at Cheshunt on Sunday 3 September 1598 led to days of drunkenness, centred on John Bull's house at Woodgreen. There was a quarrel at the fair; the trouble makers went to John Bull's house where they drank two dozen or more pots; when the quarrel continued Bull asked some drovers to leave. The rest of the crowd stayed drinking through the night and finished off another forty pots when they came downstairs on Monday morning. At William Cordle's house they drank a kilderkin, sixteen to eighteen gallons, in two hours, killed a goose, brought it to Bull's to roast, and drank another kilderkin in Bull's parlour. How six of the crowd, who took their pots on the Green and danced, managed to stay upright is a wonder. The constable on that Monday night, the 4th, heard people singing, but only found three men asleep at a table, or pretending to be, and a stranger extremely sick in bed in the parlour. At dawn on Tuesday morning the three, with three others, stood round a pikestaff on the Green at Bull's gate with six pots of drink. When asked to leave, one of the six swore he would have enough to drink as long as he lived and would marry some old hag without a tooth in her head. They drank another kilderkin and told the constable and his companion to go their ways to the JP. When someone approached them, one of the group shot at him, saying 'God's wot, let us discharge upon him for yonder cometh the enemy'.

Attacks on persons and property

Drunken disorders reveal the underlying contempt for authority. What was even more alarming for law abiding property owners was active resistance to law officers and attacks on property by the sober. On 9 September 1592 eleven women and one man from Ware attacked three constables and their two companions with staves, beating and wounding them and freeing a prisoner. This assault was probably connected with an attack on an enclosure in Broxbourne which took place two days earlier. On 7 September 1592 the hedge round a three-and-a-half acre close in Nynhoe common field in Broxbourne had been pulled down by twelve people. What makes this attack particularly interesting is that nine of the twelve people were women; the leader was Audrey Grave, a bricklayer's wife; and six of the women were servants who seem to have taken part with their mistresses' permission. Audrey had canvassed support for several days, approaching one woman while she was milking; and she had held a meeting of half a dozen neighbours to plan the attack. Robert Grave, Audrey's husband who supported his wife in her protest against enclosure, had been punished seven years earlier for offensive remarks about the Earl of Leicester and his father, the Duke of Northumberland. The twelve people involved in the assault on the Ware constables on 9 September were imprisoned for five days.

Assaults like these were not uncommon. In November 1593 the Needham family of Little Wymondley had a fight over a distraint for a debt. George Needham and another gentleman were each fined 6s.8d and three labourers 2s.6d each. On 10 December 1597 there was an incident in Cheshunt when two labourers cut down and carried off the quickset hedge round a small close and levelled the hedge bank. On 28 August 1604 an Anstey yeoman, his sister-in-law from Barkway, a Barkway innholder and other disturbers of the peace assembled, illegally, with staves and forks, broke into a close belonging to John Parker and stole a cartload of oats worth 25s. On 28 November 1604 two Tring yeomen broke into a close belonging to Henry George and destroyed 20s worth of grass. On 4 January 1605 George Masse of Waterford in Bengeo, who was described as a common night walker and breaker of hedges, broke a hedge belonging to Waterford Hall. On 7 January 1605, between 8.00 and 9.00 am, a group of labourers with swords, staves, and bows and arrows, forced their way into the house, barn and close of William Johnson of Aldbury, a cutler, and beat and wounded him until he despaired of his life. These are an almost random selection of incidents.

Surprisingly, perhaps, parsons were involved in many different kinds of disturbances. On the morning of 30 August 1593 a group of seven Aspenden men beat up the bailiffs who had arrested Ralph Tomlyn, the rector, on the order of the Queen's Bench, and freed him. Tomlyn had been accused of not conducting services. William Tomlyne, the Aston parson and presumably a relative, was accused of disturbing his neighbours with vexatious litigation. On 6 June 1589 the vicar of Great Gaddesden, with three local labourers, had broken into a close belonging to the Earl of Derby, damaged the hay crop and seriously wounded a man working for the tenant.

The most extraordinary example of violence by a parson was a personal vendetta against a woman, the wife of a tenant of the vicar of Furneux Pelham, in 1599. The 'articles of complaint – abuses and injuries offered and done to Alice Beadle, wife of John Beadle, by William Bishop clerk' outline an astonishing story. John Beadle had hired the vicarage, except for one room, its yard and the adjoining garden from the vicar. When John Beadle was away Bishop assaulted his wife on several occasions. The cause of Bishop's viciousness may have been because Beadle had bought Bishop's apple crop at a fixed price and the crop proved to be a large one. Possibly Bishop thought he had been cheated; at any rate he persuaded Alice Beadle to come to his house, showed her the large quantity of apples and then, with his father's help, beat her until she fell down. Most of the assaults occurred in the vicarage. Bishop persuaded Alice to move from the upper chamber in which she and her husband normally slept and spend a night when her husband was away in a lower chamber. He poured water on her through a funnel which he had made 'whereby she was that night altogether disappointed of her rest [and] her bedding greatly impaired'. On another occasion Bishop attacked Alice in the yard, beating her with a staff so violently that she was unable to look after herself for a fortnight. Once William Bishop assaulted Alice when she was scalding a hog in the yard; he mocked and rebuked her, grabbed the kettle full of water to scald the hog, and threw it at her. Then he hit her with the kettle until it broke and her head was split; she fell 'dead to the ground'. There were witnesses to the time when Bishop threw brickbats and stones at Alice, forcing her into the street. Francis Young gave evidence on 2 January 1600 that about a fortnight earlier, with his wife and servants, he had passed near the vicarage and seen Alice Beadle weeping and crying bitterly; she was sitting in the vicarage yard, wringing her hands in despair. She told them that Bishop had beaten her and thrown her out of the door.

William Bishop, clerk, was presented by the jury for his 'uncharitable dealings' with Alice Beadle and for fathering a child on a Furneux Pelham widow, Agnes Warren. It was said that he refused to marry her after she became pregnant for fear of losing his benefice and that he had tried to persuade her to use certain herbs to miscarry. Unfortunately we do not know what the court decided about these remarkable accusations. According to Urwick's *Nonconformity in Hertfordshire*, there were two William Bishops: the father was vicar in 1599 and deprived of his living. He was restored in 1600 but died in the same year to be succeeded by his son. If Urwick is right, it must have been the son who attacked Alice Beadle; perhaps he was his father's curate in 1599. William Bishop junior became vicar of Brent Pelham in 1614, was himself succeeded by another in Furneux Pelham in 1615, and deprived of his Brent Pelham living in 1630, 'the cause . . . not discovered'.[7] This is all rather puzzling as is the apparent inactivity and silence of Alice's husband, John Beadle, at least as far as the records go.

Seditious and traitorous talk

The authorities feared outbreaks of violence, which could become riots, not merely because they threatened property but because they might become a danger to the state. The court records reveal undercurrents of hostility to the established Anglican church, to the monarch – the head of the church –, and to those in authority, locally and nationally. There was a continuous trickle of prosecutions for seditious speech which often took the form of criticisms of the doctrines of the Anglican church. Recusants, men and women who refused to attend Anglican church services though bound by law to do so, survived through Queen Elizabeth I's reign and into the seventeenth century. Over sixty such recusants appeared before the Hertfordshire courts between 1575 and 1625. Thirty of them lived in the east of the county, in an area bounded by Barkway, Furneux Pelham, Bishops Stortford, Sawbridgeworth, Hunsdon, Stanstead Abbots, Bramfield, Aston, and Westmill. There were many married couples, and a few large families. There were 30 ordinary working people: 7 yeomen, 1 husbandman, 2 labourers, 8 women, and 7 tradesmen or craftsmen – a barber, a blacksmith, a joiner, a mercer, a wheelwright, and 2 carpenters. Five people had no special description. Just over half of the total were from titled or gentry families, two of whom, the Fosters of Hunsdon and Marmaduke Tirwhitt of Ippollitts, sheltered socially more vulnerable fellow believers.

It is too often assumed that all recusants were Roman Catholics; this is unlikely to be true of Hertfordshire. Hunsdon and its neighbour, Widford, were Puritan centres and it is probable that the Fosters, who were regularly presented for not attending church between 1615 and 1625, were Puritans and sheltering Puritans. Thomas Foster's wife, Mary, was one of several gentry wives whose newborn children were not baptised. There is no doubt about the Puritanism of four people from Great and Little Gaddesden who were brought before Assizes between 1607 and 1614: Henry Pratt, a carpenter, and his wife, John Gefferie, a wheelwright, and John Rutland, another carpenter. Pratt was described in 1607 as a Brownist and a Recusant. Brownists were the later Independents – Congregationalists. We have a pen picture of an aggressive local Puritan in 1589. John Carter, tailor of St Albans, broke into conversation between the vicars of Ippollitts, Offley, and Great Wymondley in Hitchin market place. John Stratts of Ippollitts reproved Carter: 'my friend, you profess yourself a scholar; you should learn better manners than to come to hear men's counsel before you be called', to which Carter replied 'thou art a dumb dog and a cur'. Roger Henlaye of Offley rejoined: 'it becomes thee not to use these speeches; he is thy better', to which Carter replied, monotonously, 'thou art a dumb dog and a cur too'. Earlier Carter had reproved the Hitchin minister, Mr Chambers, for using prayers in church on Wednesdays and Fridays without preaching as well, a typical Puritan point of view. Robert Warren, the Hitchin clerk, was called a 'half face priest' for suggesting that Carter might talk to the minister privately.

Puritan critics used the bible to criticise the queen and the clergy. John Este, a Hemel Hempstead yeoman, was imprisoned for six months in 1576 for defaming the book of common prayer by denying that 'if a godly prince do command . . . we must obey . . . for David caused Urias to be set in the forefront of the battle whereby David did wickedly and all they that did obey him'. In 1589 the parson of Hinxworth, John Mychelie, said that Hezekiah when taxed by Assyria paid from his own coffers, 'but princes nowadays . . . keep their own coffers full and lay it upon the commonalty'. While John Hale, a Hatfield yeoman, argued in 1590 'that the Church of England was no true nor lawful Church nor the Ministers of the Church of England are no lawful ministers of the Church of Christ. And that he cannot tell whether the Queens Majesty be a true, lawful and christian magistrate, but he thinketh Her Majesty is a lawful governor.' Thomas Hale, a Welwyn tanner and, presumably, a relative, added that the Church's ministers 'were all ministers of the false church because they are called by bishops which are Antichristian. And that it is as lawful for a thief to take a purse by the highway side as a minister to claim tithes'. The nub of the matter was made clear in an accusation made in 1589 that the minister of Nazeing in Essex had said in Hertfordshire that 'there is no supreme head under God but the minister'. He actually said 'there ought to be no supreme head under God but the queen and the minister'. Puritan maybe but not seditious, as was the earlier version. The same distinction appears in the prosecution of Roman Catholics. At the 1605 Assizes John Clarke, a Stepney clothworker, admitted saying at Aldenham that 'the English bible now used in the Church of England is not truly translated according to the Latin . . . the ministers . . . at the present day are not true ministers of the Church of God,. . . he will not come into the church where they do say prayers or minister sacraments'. Significantly, he was discharged when he took the oath of supremacy although he said he would die in 'the Romish religion'. At the same Assizes Robert Bastard, a Roman Catholic yeoman from Hertford, took the opposite view. He confessed that he had denied the royal supremacy because 'he doth confidently believe the Roman Church to be the true Catholic Church'. Only those ultramontane Catholics who believed the pope could depose monarchs were treated as traitors. The others were punished as recusants for not attending church.

The mystique of the universally adored Queen Elizabeth I supported by a Protestant people united in a xenophobic hatred of Spain, has sunk so deeply into people's minds that it may still surprise some readers to learn that at least three Hertfordshire inhabitants, from different parts of the county, welcomed a Spanish invasion in 1596. Their sympathy with the Roman Catholic enemy, whose second Armada was preparing to sail, was revealingly linked with hostility to some of the new rich Hertfordshire gentry. John Feere, an Albury brickmaker, was accused of saying publicly at Thundridge: 'I would that all the Spaniards of Spain were landed here in England to pull out the boors and churls by the ears; and that twenty thousand of them were about Mr Capell's house (meaning Arthur Capel of Little Hadham esq.,), for then he would turn unto them and should be much set by'. Robert Nicholls, a Watford baker, said: 'There was reason every man should have his right (referring to Philip, King of Spain), for it was his due to have the third foot of England by marrying with our last queen (meaning Mary, late Queen of England), and that every man would seek for his own'. While Roger Sly or Slyford, a Hertford gentleman, claimed: 'That now the Spaniards would shortly come amongst us, whereby he hoped to see such rule in England as he should domineer over that knave Ralph Coningsby'.

The Armada threat produced a scandalous rumour of negligence in high quarters. Charles, Baron Howard of Effingham, Lord High Admiral, had commanded the fleet which met the Armada in 1588; in 1596 he raided Cadiz with Essex and was made Earl of Nottingham. Edward Bull and Edward Whytenbury, a tailor, claimed they had heard Thomas Antwissel, who had recently been to Court, stating on Cottered Green that Howard had put sand instead of powder into the barrels for Essex's ships. When examined, Antwissel 'confessed that he told Whytenbury that there was sand or grease where powder should be, but . . . not by the Lord Admiral's means'.

Seditious talk could aim higher. In 1585 Robert Grave of Broxbourne, whose wife organised an enclosure protest seven years later, had been punished for saying 'when the Duke of Northumberland was overcome by Queen Mary there were very great bonfires made in Ware'. The Duke's son was Queen Elizabeth's favourite, the Earl of Leicester. This was why Grave's next remarks were so offensive: he said that the 'duke was a traitorous villain and all they that came of him never were good to England nor never would be'. Another attack on the Earl of Leicester was made by one of three vagrants who were put in the pillory in 1592 with papers on their heads describing their offences. The vagrant had said that it was well known to the Queen's Council that the earl was a traitor. When he returned from Flanders with the Earl of Derby, he had brought with him a 'scroll' of his treason 'to the length of half a yard'. Such outspoken, blunt attacks on the queen's servants led to attacks on the government and the queen herself. In 1585 John Grene, a Hertford labourer, had said in public 'that the Council, meaning the queen's most honourable Council, have no more mercy than a dog', for which piece of impertinence he was whipped and put in the pillory. So was Thomas Boraston or Levaston, an Aldenham yeoman, for slanderous words against the queen in 1591; from the pillory he went to prison. Agnes Lewes of Harpenden was accused of slandering Parliament in 1598. In 1601 Nicholas Welch, a Cheshunt gentleman, was hung for telling George Hayes: 'I hope to see thee hanged, and the queen too, yea by God's wounds, in chains'.

Only seven days after Queen Elizabeth's death, a Buntingford grocer, Thomas Browne said: 'we who looked for the queen's death these twenty years will not be made fools of now . . . a Scot [James VI and I] should not wear the Crown of England . . . although all the men of England would join with the king, yet he would be against him'. Browne added that he would tell the king when he came 'that he was come into a place whereof he was not worthy'.

Browne believed that the rightful heir to the throne was Henry VII's great-great-grandson, Edward, illegitimate son of Catherine and Edward Seymour, Earl of Hertford. Catherine was Lady Jane Grey's sister and the earl was Jane Seymour's nephew. The earl 'was ready in the West country with thirty thousand men' said Browne and he, Browne, 'had armour of his own to furnish five men, and . . . would procure one thousand men more to join with the earl against the king'. Thomas Browne was found to be guilty but remanded without sentence. 'Traitorous words' were used by Oliver Bayneham of Hoddesdon as late as 1616. The degree of dissatisfaction with the social order, which lay behind some at least, of this seditious talk, was revealed in June 1602 by John Tompson, a Much Hadham labourer. He was arrested as a vagrant soldier who had failed to return to and take up employment in his place of settlement. After his arrest he said 'that if he were at liberty again as he had been, he would never betray man while he lived; and that if he were a soldier again as he had been, he would rather fight against his country than with it'.

Witchcraft

How far, and in what ways if any, witchcraft was connected with hostility to the establishment is unclear. It cannot be entirely a coincidence that accusations of witchcraft were made predominantly in the same areas as those in which recusancy flourished and in Cheshunt, a centre of vagrancy and misbehaviour in alehouses. There was certainly an element of spite, reflections of tensions in local communities, but some people accused of witchcraft were involved in various forms of protest against authority. Examples are the Brownes of Buntingford and the Whitenburys of Cottered. Witchcraft was essentially a female crime and one of which spinsters in particular were accused. There were 49 witchcraft cases between 1573 and 1621: 11 south and east of Bengeo and Hertford, 4 of which were in Cheshunt; 17 east of a line from Ashwell down the river Beane to Hertford, of which 2 each were in Ashwell, Aspenden, Barkway, Buntingford and Royston; but only 12 west of the Lea and Hertford, 4 of which were in Flamstead and Great Gaddesden. The Brownes of Buntingford were accused both of treason and witchcraft. Thomas' treasonable statements in 1601 we have seen. Elleñ or Helen, a spinster described as of Aspenden and of Buntingford, was accused between 1588 and 1593 of several offences of bewitching cattle and people. She spent a year in prison and when discharged in March 1591 was put in the pillory. When accused again in 1593 she was acquitted, as was William, a Buntingford locksmith, accused of bewitching a local man on 16 December 1598. A William Browne, yeoman of Westmill, and Thomas Browne, baker of Barkway, were sureties for his appearance; was this the seditious Thomas of 1601? Was the vagrant Richard Emes who was put in the pillory in 1592 for his accusations against the Earl of Leicester related to Alice Eames, who was accused of bewitching cattle in 1594? Thomas Antwissel nurtured his quarrel with Edward Whitenbury of Cottered from 1596 to 1618 when he accused Edward Whitenbury of witchcraft; Whitenbury was only delivered from gaol by Proclamation. Between 1601 and 1603 another Whitenbury, Agnes wife of Robert of Aston, had actually been found guilty of bewitching to death two piglets.

The really terrible thing is that of the fifty-five people accused of witchcraft, forty-three were women, of whom twenty-three were found guilty and nine hung. Only six of the fifteen accused wives were found guilty, but eleven of fourteen accused spinsters. Only three of the thirteen accused men were found guilty and one was hung. Two Royston women, probably sisters, Christian and Alice Stokes were hung for murders by witchcraft which they were supposed to have committed between 1593 and 1606. They were both spinsters, typical scapegoats. In Ashwell a widow, Agnes Smith, was acquitted of bewitching horses and people, some of whom died, between 1605 and 1611. An Anne Smith, also a widow, served the statutory year in prison followed by pillory, for bewitching a man and a horse in 1614-15. They may well have been the same person. Some spinsters, who were found guilty, were saved the worst penalties by ingenious court decisions. Agnes Morris of Stevenage was found guilty of bewitching Robert Jenkinson on 1 July 1582 so that he languished until 1 May 1583 and died, but she was remanded after sentence had been passed because the evidence was weak. In 1600-1 Mercy Hills of Barley was found guilty of trespass not murder, although two women and a black cow had died. Sarah Asser of Little Munden, accused of murder by witchcraft in 1601, was found guilty only of stealing an ash cloth worth 10d!

The most common cases of witchcraft were 19 of bewitching animals, 15 of making people ill so that they 'languished', and 32 of killing people. Many people were accused of several different offences. The

51 pigs, 13 horses, 8 cows and, in two cases, cattle supposedly bewitched between 1575 and 1618 do not seem so many if we think of the innumerable premature animal deaths which malice or superstition could have blamed on witches. Alice Cowle, a Therfield spinster, was sentenced to be put in the pillory for six hours on four occasions in 1575, 'to confess her offence', which was bewitching a brewing vat full of water at which Henry Gynne's two cows were drinking, though no evidence was given that the cows suffered. In 1590 a Bengeo spinster, Mary Burgis, was found guilty of making George Grave's arm lame; in 1598 a Barkway labourer was accused of making a left leg lame; in 1600 the wife of a Chipping Barnet barber, accused of bewitching the back of the head of a sixteen year old girl so that she died, was acquitted. Alexander Lewis of St Albans was accused of enchantments and poisoning gloves in 1609. In seven cases between 1604 and 1621 the accusation was of suspicion of witchcraft without details being given.

Three 'white' witches were quite different from all the others. They were part cheating hucksters, part fortune tellers, and part purveyors of 'alternative' medicine. On 1 January 1573 a Hoddesdon yeoman, Thomas Heather, conjured spirits – his sixteenth century metal detector – to help him find money in a wood. Both the other two white witches came from the Hitchin area: Thomas Harding of Ickleford in 1589-90 and Elizabeth Lane, widow of Walsworth, in 1597. Three people had asked Harding to find stolen goods, two people consulted him over illness, and one to find out 'who had fired his mother's house at Weston'. Eleven people, all from Guilden Morden in Cambridgeshire, consulted Elizabeth, five about illness, three about theft, and three about Grace Lilley though what was wrong with her is not recorded. None of them got any satisfaction. Harding was certainly ingenious: in one case he said that the thief would come into the house with a feather through her nose, but no one came. Mary Pennyfeather of Ippollitts, whose child 'could neither go nor speak', was first told her child was a changeling, then told to fill a nut with quicksilver and put it under the child's pillow, and finally told to put the child in a chair on her dung hill for an hour on a sunny day. None of these cures by Harding worked. The 'scroll of parchment' with 'certain words' which another patient was told to hang round his neck was more conventional, but the patient died. In most of the cases of illness brought to Elizabeth Lane she blamed John Knightley, the vicar of Guilden Morden: one man possessed by spirits was bewitched by the minister; another man's wife was bewitched by deep and profane learning; and a woman's husband was 'beworded and bewatled' by John Knightley. 'Bewatled' came from wattle which meant a coxcomb or show off. The bewatled husband died although his wife had faithfully carried out the witch's instructions, to cut off his hair and send it to the witch, turn his bed round, and throw his water into the fire. Needless to say most of these poor supplicants had paid for the useless advice they received: sums of money – 6d, 1s, 2s, and even £2 with £20 promised – bacon, pigeons, cheese.

Witchcraft, black and white, was as much a rejection of the established order as recusancy. In their different ways all those described in this chapter were social outcasts. Vagrants and mothers of illegitimate children, lewd men, thieves and murderers, gamblers, drunkards and rioters, those who would not attend their parish church and spouters of sedition were, all alike, unwanted by the 'good and able subjects' of the 1598 Poor Law. Yet they were 'not nothing'; they were a part of local society in the past and their presence should not be forgotten as the lives of more fortunate people are explored in what follows.

NOTES

1 Walt Whitman *Leaves of Grass* Siegle, Hill & Co. London (1907), p 390

2 Lothrop Withington, ed., *Elizabethan England* pp 122-4

3 Quoted in Maurice Bruce *The Coming of the Welfare State* (1968) p 36

4 Unless otherwise stated, all quotations and cases cited come from two sources:
        Assize Records: J S Cockburn has edited two calendar volumes – *Calendar of Assize Records – Hertfordshire Indictments. Elizabeth I*; and ditto *James I*;
  and: Quarter Sessions Records: two published volumes concern the period covered – *Hertfordshire County Records. Vol I Notes and Extracts from the Sessions Rolls 1581-1698* compiled by W J Hardy; *Vol V Calendar to the Sessions Books and other Sessions Records 1619-57* compiled by William Le Hardy.
Manuscript calendars for the years 1588-1619 are in HCR0.

5 Hon. Herbert Cokayne Gibbs *The Parish Registers of Hunsdon 1546-1837* pp 101, 68, 70, 74, 111.

6 *Shakespeare's England* Vol II, (1916, reprinted 1950) pp 484-5.

7 William Urwick *Nonconformity in Hertfordshire* (1884) pp 763 & 761.

~2~
'GOD IN HIS GOOD TIME RESTORE THE VULGAR PEOPLE TO THEIR FORMER OBEDIENCE' 1660-1688

During the Civil War, Commonwealth and Protectorate, social outcasts like those described in the previous chapter surfaced to such an extent that one historian of the period has written of *The world turned upside down.*[1] The Restoration of Charles II has been, almost universally, described as though it was an occasion of general rejoicing. So it was for very many, in particular the many who had been seriously disturbed by the social and religious changes of the previous twenty years. In August 1649 Dame Anne Sadleir of the Standon family left her books and coins to Trinity College, Cambridge. The

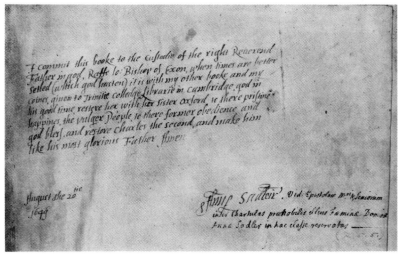

Plate 2 Inscription from Dame Anne Sadleir's copy of the *Apocalypse,* which she left to Trinity College Cambridge in 1649. [Reproduced by kind permission of the Master and Fellows of Trinity College, Cambridge].

inscription in the *Apocalypse* reads: 'God in his good time restore her [Cambridge] with her Sister Oxford to there pristine happines, the Vulger People to there former obedience, and God bless and restore Charles the Second and make him like his most glorious Father. Amen.'[2] One of God's instruments in achieving Anne Sadleir's prayers was Sir Harbottle Grimston, owner in 1660 of the Bacons' Gorhambury. Sir Harbottle had been an active member of the Long Parliament in its early years, opposing Charles I's government, but never happy with the religious and democratic views of the sects. He was one of the Presbyterian MPs ejected from the Commons in Pride's Purge in 1648. He was elected to Cromwell's second parliament in 1656 but was not permitted to take his seat. He was one of the excluded members of the Long Parliament who returned in February 1660. He was elected to the Convention Parliament and chosen Speaker when it met on 25 April 1660. As Speaker he went to Breda to invite Charles II to return; for his part in the Restoration he was made Master of the Rolls. Sir Harbottle Grimston's attitude to the 'vulgar people' is revealed in a fascinating diary which he kept of 'Three weeks' observations of the States Countreys, especially Holland'. He was more ambivalent than Dame Anne Sadleir, clearly admiring many aspects of Dutch society, but he also disliked the disobedience of vulgar people. 'Their government is a democracy, and there had need be many to rule such a rabble of rude ones. Tell them of a king and they could cut your throat in earnest; . . . None among them hath authority by inheritance; . . . they are all chosen as we choose aldermen, more for their wealth than their wit, . . . There is not under heaven such a den of several serpents as Amsterdam is; . . . 'Tis an university of all opinions which grow here confusedly, . . If you be unsettled in your religion, you may here try all . . . If you fancy none, you have a pattern to follow . . . In their families they are all equals, and you have no way to know the master and mistress but by taking them in bed together.'[3]

The Restoration united for a time the Grimstons and those who saw the world like Anne Sadleir but there were many who thought differently and some who suffered. Daniel Axtell of Berkhamsted became an apprentice in London where he joined the parliamentary armies when the Civil War began and rose to become a lieutenant-colonel in the New Model Army. He commanded the guards at Charles I's trial and because of this was executed at the Restoration. In prison, preparing for death, he spoke of 'that Good Old Cause which we were

Plate 3 Daniel Axtell. From Clarendon's *History of the Rebellion* vol 6 [British Museum].

engaged in, under the parliament; I am now going to be their martyr'. When asked 'what he meant by the Cause' Col. Axtell replied, 'Sir, I tell you, I mean that Cause which we were encouraged to, and engaged in under parliament, which was for common Right and Freedom, and against the Surplice and Common Prayer Book'.[4] Not all the 'vulgar people' were restored 'to their former obedience'. In 1660 Robert Hart, a Thundridge shoemaker, told the newly appointed Anglican vicar of Standon: 'Thou art a drunkard, swearer, liar, sabbath breaker, no minister of Jesus Christ, but a greedy dog, a preacher of lies and a leader of people into darkness'. As for Charles II's right to rule as king, the shoemaker 'knew no power but God's, neither would he submit to any other power, the rest were but men and all alike in power'.[5]

What had happened during the Interregnum was that disrespect for the established order of society, which had always existed among sections of the common people, had been widely and publicly expressed taking on religious and political forms. It was this which the Restoration establishment feared and repressed. However Axtell's Cause did not die at the Restoration, anymore than Hart's social contempt for authority, but they went underground. For something like twenty years the activity of local religious dissenters provided a focus for discontent and supplied a continuing example of how to organise and how to express anti-authoritarian ideas. There was a close connection, almost an identity, between religious, social, and political nonconformity, as Axtell's and Hart's words reveal. The study of local dissent between 1660 and 1688 helps to explain the outburst of publicly expressed social and political criticism in the 1680s.

Dissent in Hertfordshire

Oliver Cromwell argued that 'notions will hurt none but those that have them'. In 1656 he said 'our practice hath been to let all this nation see that whatever pretensions to religion would continue quiet and peaceable, they should enjoy conscience and liberty to themselves'.[6] The parliaments of the restored Stuarts thought differently and in the Clarendon Code (1661-5) did their best to destroy religious dissent. Only in 1672 and 1687-8, when Charles II and James II issued Declarations of Indulgence, were those who did not accept the tenets and practices of the Anglican church free to follow their own forms of worship. After the accession of William III and Mary II an Act of Toleration became law. As James Wittewronge wrote to his father, Sir John, the seventy-one year old owner of Rothamsted and one-time MP in Cromwell's parliament: 'yesterday the Parliament was upon the bill about religion, and have voted what I have often heard you say viz: that those only shall be punished that do not go to church, or to some other public meeting where God is worshipped, and it shall be at everyone's liberty where they will go'.[7] After 1689 not going to church, or drinking during the time of church services, might be an offence but it was no longer equated with political disaffection. Before 1687 it was. Thus Daniel Skingle and James Gatward of Great Munden were bound over in 1685 as 'notorious Dissenters and utterly disaffected to the government'. Thomas Wilson, the Munden curate gave evidence that they had not been seen at divine service. Skingle's name appears in a list 'of the members of the Congregational Church at Hartford which began in the year 1673' and against his name is written 'his gift of prophecying or preaching approved of by the church, and prayed for and allowed of with a promise of leaving his calling and giving himself wholly to it'.[8] By their regular holding of public meetings, 'preachifyings', even in the open air, the Dissenters must have encouraged others to express all kinds of critical views. At least this is what the authorities feared: in 1669 Quarter Sessions were told that there were 'frequent unlawful assemblies of great numbers of persons, both at Theobalds, and at the houses commonly called the King's Stables and elsewhere, in the parish of Cheshunt to the terror of the King's subjects'. The Quakers held open-air conventicles in the street of Hoddesdon in 1684 and 1685.

Dissent was strong in Hertfordshire in the years 1660 to 1688. The Compton Return of 1676 lists 1,890 Dissenters and 74 Roman Catholics in the county, just over 11% of the recorded adults. One-third of the adults in Hertford, one-quarter in four parishes round Hitchin, and just over one-fifth in five contiguous parishes including Berkhamsted and Hemel Hempstead, were Dissenters.[9] The return almost certainly underestimates the real numbers in some parishes. There was a flourishing Quaker meeting in Baldock, to judge from Quarter Sessions records, but the Compton Return is of forty-five Roman Catholics and only fourteen Dissenters out of 495 adults. The Catholics are probably a mistake. Only sixty-three Dissenters out of 506 adults were returned in Cheshunt, but the Quarter Sessions records name between 90 and 100 Cheshunt inhabitants as attending unlawful conventicles and/or as among 'the wealthiest Dissenters in the parish' in 1682-3 and something like a further thirty are named as not attending church between 1663 and 1675; there must have been others unnamed. William Urwick's *Nonconformity in Herts.* (1884) has a great deal of information about Dissenters in most areas of the county, and Violet Rowe, in *The First Hertford Quakers* (1970), has studied one 'Meeting' in detail. An exploration of the activities of Quakers in Baldock and of various Dissenters in Cheshunt and the surrounding area may serve, as examples, to show how local groups of believers persisted in public defiance of the penal Clarendon Code. Their defiance must have been contagious, spreading awareness of the possibility, and even the desirability, of challenging authority.

The Quakers in Baldock

George Fox recorded a visit to Baldock in 1655 where he healed a sick Baptist woman: 'Her husband's name was (Thomas) Baldock. . . this Baptist woman and her husband came to be convinced; and many hundreds of people have there been at meetings at their house since, and great meetings and convincement there was up and down in those parts'. Fox returned in 1668: 'I went to Baldock where I had a great meeting of many hundreds of people of many sorts'.[10] From the Quarter Sessions records and from Besse's *Sufferings* we know of some of the Baldock meetings which the authorities persecuted. On 13 January 1660 'a constable, with many rude attendants, rushed into the meeting at Baldock, and after many blows and abuses forcibly dragged out' seventeen people 'whom they kept all night at an inn without beds, and next day carried them to Hertford, . . where they were committed to the county jail'.[11] There was a meeting at Thomas Baldock's house on 31 July 1664, attended by twenty-five people. William and Thomas Burr were fined in 1670 for meetings held in their houses, Thomas 'for four several meetings at his house'. In 1675 thirty-one people were convicted of assembling, on various occasions between 5 March and 4 April, at their Meeting-house in Baldock, under the colour of exercising religion in other manner than according to the liturgy of the Church of England.

These meetings were recorded because the authorities punished people who attended, by fines or imprisonment. When fines were not paid, goods were distrained. Many of the Baldock Quakers were maltsters and brewers. Their malt was distrained for unpaid fines. William Burr was fined £20 on 12 May 1670; Thomas, on 17 June, 'suffered the spoiling of his goods to the value of £130'. Local law officers 'broke open his malt-house, and carried away one hundred and four quarters of malt'. Significantly twenty-six quarters of confiscated malt 'was put in the market-house because no person in the town would receive it'. The Baldock constables reported in 1675 that 'they took away from the Quakers for their meeting' the following goods: '2 pair of shoes 5s, 2 bushel of malt 5s, 1 dozen of candles 4s.6d, 6 pair of stockings 5s. . . here is all that we could come at for all the gates and doors were all lockt'. None of the goods, which were sold on 23 March 1676, were bought for the prices they had been valued at: shoes 4s, malt 4s, candles 3s.6d, and stockings 4s. In 1684 goods worth £74.8s.9d were distrained from six people for non-payment of fines.

Fines and confiscation of goods were not the only punishments inflicted for persisting in holding meetings. Ironically the two Burrs were in gaol when fined in 1670; along with Lewis Laundy and Thomas Mosse – and Henry Stout of Hertford – they had been sentenced, in October 1664, to seven years banishment in Jamaica for taking part in the meeting in Thomas Baldock's house in the previous

July. Only 'after eight years of confinement under sentence of trans-portation were [they] by the Kings Letters Patent at length dis-charged from their long captivity in the County gaol at Hertford'. In 1674 John Mosse was sent to prison 'for not paying towards repairs of the Steeple House'. Between 1682 and 1685 Lewis Laundy, Thomas Baldock, Thomas and John Mosse, and Anthony, Edward and Thomas Fage were in and out of prison for refusing to take the oath of alle-giance. These men and the Burrs, and their families, were the core of the enduring Baldock Quaker organisation. Thomas Baldock, his wife and daughter were regularly in conflict with authority between 1660 and 1685; five Burrs obstinately refused to conform at different dates between 1658 and 1682, three Fages between 1675 and 1685, three Laundys between 1664 and 1686, and three Mosses between 1664 and 1686. That the county authorities thought these Baldock Quakers were a potential political threat appeared in 1685, in the 'time of the rebellion of the Duke of Monmouth', when Thomas Baldock, Thomas and John Mosse, and Anthony and Thomas Fage appeared before the Midsummer Quarter Sessions as 'disaffected persons to the govern-ment'. With typical Quaker persistence, they refused to be bound over for their good behaviour and refused to take the oath of alle-giance.

There is one almost certain link between the Baldock Meeting and the Ware area. Thomas Burr is not recorded in Baldock after 1670 but in 1670, 'Thomas Burr, to whom a lease of the Meeting-house at Ware was conveyed, was, for several meetings there, fined £20 each time, and had his goods taken by several distresses within this year, to the value of £101.14s'. Thereafter Thomas Burr of Ware, maltster, was reg-ularly in trouble until 1685.

Dissent in the area of Cheshunt

In the area south of Ware there was considerable support not only for Quakers but also for Baptists, Independents, and Presbyterians. Many of these congregations were regional, drawing in supporters from a wide area. Gawen Lowry's QUAKER Meeting at Flamstead End in 1683 had over 100 people in attendance: thirty-four from Cheshunt, twenty-six from Waltham Abbey, thirteen from Hoddesdon, eleven from Enfield, three each from Edmonton, Epping, London, and Northaw, two from Broxbourne, and one each from Nazeing and Roydon, Berkshire and Montgomery. John Knight's parallel Quaker Meeting in Hoddesdon in the same year was attended by over fifty people: eleven from Hoddesdon, six from Great Amwell, five from Waltham Abbey, four from each of Cheshunt, Roydon, and Ware, three from each of Broxbourne and Little Amwell, two from each of Harlow, Hertford and London, and one from each of Eastwick, Epping, Hunsdon, Standon and Theydon Garnon. Five people from

Hoddesdon, one from Broxbourne and one from Waltham Abbey were at both meetings. There were twenty-six women and twenty-five men at John Knight's meeting.

Thomas Burr, the Ware maltster who had moved from Baldock, seems to have been a peripatetic teacher. In 1675 he was convicted of attending a conventicle at Roydon and fined. In 1683 he was fined £20 for teaching at a conventicle at Patmore Heath in Albury. Besse states that 'Thomas Burr of Ware, for being at two meetings, had taken from him 26 quarters of malt worth £26.18s'. The Ware constables reported on 14 July that this malt was 'still on their hands to their great damage for shop rent, they having made an outcry for the sale of the same, and nobody will give any money for it'. Burr's gelding, seized 'for a seditious conventicle and meeting held in the street of Broxbourne . . ., in like manner nobody would buy'. Not only were the Quakers so popular locally that nobody wanted to buy their distrained goods, they were also strong enough and bold enough to hold open-air meetings. On Sunday 17 February 1684 Knight's Quakers held a conventicle 'in the open street or highway' in Hoddesdon; this was the meeting attended by Thomas Burr. On 2 August 1685 the local Quaker conventicle met partly in John Knight's barn or outhouse and partly in the open street adjoining. Another unlawful assembly was held in the street on 25 October 1685.

While Thomas Burr was a maltster, the other leading local Quakers followed different occupations: Nicholas King (or Ring) of Cheshunt was a bricklayer, John Knight of Hoddesdon a hatter, Gawen Lowry or Lourdy, variously identified as 'speaker', preacher or teacher of the Flamstead End Meeting, was at one time described as a labourer, at another as a merchant. How reliable these descriptions are one cannot be sure: Nicholas King was presented in 1666 'for suffering marriages to be solemnized in his house; also for suffering corpses of dead folks to be interred in his garden or orchard'.[12] However in 1685 Nicholas was listed with six others as 'all poor and nothing to be had' by way of fine or distress; but in 1688 he was one of the Cheshunt surveyors, presented 'for not repairing the highway'. Because some of the lists of those attending Quaker meetings give occupations we have a suggestion as to the social structure of the Cheshunt, Hoddesdon and Patmore Heath Meetings. There were three gentlemen, one yeoman, one merchant, three malsters or maltmakers, one mealman, one petty chapman, five husbandmen, and six labourers. There were twenty-three craftsmen: four shoemakers (cordwainers), four weavers one of whom was a woman and one a silkweaver, three bricklayers, two coopers, two tanners, and one each of the following trades: chandler, draper, grocer, hatter, shopkeeper, tailor, wheelwright, and woolcomber. One interesting Quaker was Matthew Orgar, summoned before the justices for attending the Flamstead End conventicle in 1683, who produced a certificate on 1 October: he 'is wondrous old, nearly ninety years, troubled with falling fits, almost blind, very deaf, and unable to wait on you in person. Therefore, we humbly request that you will not look on him as a contemnor of authority but rather as bis puer', in other words in his second childhood.

Persecution was almost as prevalent as in Baldock. Nicholas King, who housed the Cheshunt Meeting, was prosecuted in every year from 1660 to 1664 and imprisoned in April 1666. In 1675, 1679, 1682, 1683 and 1685 he was in some kind of trouble or other. Non-attendance at church and non-payment of tithes were the most common offences, in addition to attending conventicles for which William Bates, a silkweaver, and his wife, Robert Cocke, Robert Cooper, Robert and, later, widow Sarah Runnington, were persistently prosecuted in the 1660s and 1670s. In 1683 John Knight was fined £20 for organising the Hoddesdon conventicle, and those attending were fined 5s each.

In 1685 Thomas Burr and William Simson of Amwell suffered distress 'to the value of £41.3s . . . for their religious meetings'. As late as 10 May 1689 Burr was committed to Hertford gaol at the suit of the Ware parson 'for a claim of small tithes'. 'Corn, grass, household goods, and other things worth £8.6s.11d' were taken from Burr and three other people. John Fisher, described as a gentleman, was a schoolmaster who belonged to the Hoddesdon Meeting. In 1679 he was presented 'for not coming to church three Sundays' and in February 1682 presented because he kept a school for teaching boys without a licence from the Bishop of London. In October 1682 he was imprisoned for refusing to take the oath of allegiance; he was still refusing to take the oath in July 1684, and still in prison in January 1686.

The most vicious piece of local persecution of the Cheshunt Quakers is described by Besse. In 1682 two local JPs levied £120 in distresses for meetings: £33 was levied on Nicholas King, Nathaniel Tomson, John Roberts, John Blinden, and Richard Saunder; £87 on William Bilton, William Wild, Thomas Watson, John Bowman, and the widow Runnington. In October 1682 further goods, to the value of £31.0s.8d, were taken from Gawen Lowry, Wonderful Warwick and Thomas Roberts. Not content with this the JPs set about destroying the Flamstead End Meeting-house. Benches and forms, the galleries, windows, doors and walls were broken up, and the chimney piece caught fire. There followed an incident which revealed the local divide that religious persecution had produced, and the willingness to stand up and oppose authority which Quaker defiance helped to strengthen among ordinary people. A poor man called John Parsons was ordered by a JP to assist in the demolition but he refused. When threatened he replied: 'I am contented, Sir, if I must go to gaol for not working on Sundays', which effectively ended the JP's threats. Needless to say the destruction of the Meeting-house did not end the Cheshunt conventicle: Nicholas King and Gawen Lowry were both teaching in 1683.

The local BAPTIST conventicle at Theobalds in Cheshunt went back, at least, to 1658 when the Protectorate Council had approved 'Captain' John Spencer as 'preacher at Theobalds' and augmented his salary by £50 pa.[13] Spencer appeared, intermittently, in the Quarter Sessions' records between 1664 and 1682. In 1669 he was the preacher of a Hertford 'meeting of Anabaptists to the number of four hundred and upward'.[14] In 1671 he had to produce sureties 'to answer for being a person of evil conversation, a rioter and a perturber of His Majesty's peace'. 'Conversation' in the seventeenth century had the meanings 'having dealings with others' and 'behaviour, mode or course of life'.[15] By 1672, if not before, Spencer was back in Cheshunt. Charles II's Declaration of Indulgence, temporarily, legalised Dissent, and John Spencer was licensed 'to be a Baptist teacher in the house of Anthony Spinage' of Cheshunt. Spinage's house was licensed for Baptist worship on 25 July.[16]

But this freedom did not last. In 1681 Spencer had to produce sureties for good behaviour; he was described as 'an idle, dissolute and lewd fellow, refusing to put himself out to service, liveth and spendeth high, keeping many horses, and not having any visible means to do the same'. In 1682 he was named as one 'of the wealthiest Dissenters in the parish of Cheshunt . . . Such as are Anabaptists.' He was one of their two 'Teachers'; the other was Mr Joseph Masters.

This was the only occasion when Masters appeared in the Quarter Sessions records, but Urwick has an account of his life. In 1661 he left Magdalen Hall [now Hertford College], Oxford because of his 'nonconforming to the ecclesiastical discipline lately introduced into the said college'. 'He settled with a worshipping society of Christians at Theobalds . . . and was ordained . . . October 30th 1667'. In 1672 he was licensed as 'a Baptist general teacher' and remained at Theobalds until about 1690 when he was invited to become elder of a rich London congregation. For some twenty more years he came to Theobalds once a month to preach to the Theobalds congregation which had been 'reduced to a very small number, and met in a Presbyterian meeting-house, the ministers of the two congregations dividing the work'.[17] Urwick mentions another local Baptist, Major Richard Woollaston, Cromwell's gunfounder, who 'purchased half the manor of Wormley about 1656'. The County histories and Dorothy Bushby and William Le Hardy's *Wormley in Hertfordshire* all put Woollaston's purchase at a much later date. This may explain why Woollaston does not appear to have been indicted in Hertfordshire. There is no mention of him in the Sessions Records, although he was described as 'by persuasion an Anabaptist (I think or very near it) and one that was frequently troubled with indictments and informations for not going to church and for going to conventicles, by Sir Henry Wroth, the Lord Fanshawe, etc.'.[18] There was a small conventicle in Wormley, however, which met in the house of Henry Pank who seems to have come from Ware. He was described as a Ware linendraper in 1662 but as a maltster in 1667 when he was presented for not attending church. In 1670 he was sent to gaol until he found sureties for good behaviour; his wife who had also been gaoled was released. Then in 1679 he and his wife were each fined 5s, as were three other people, because they had attended a conventicle in Henry Pank's house in Wormley.

The most extraordinary character who, for a time at least, was a Baptist and who lived in Cheshunt was Thomas Medlicot. Prosecuted for non-attendance at church in 1661, 1670 and 1682 in which year he headed a list of ten people who 'seldom go to church or any other religious meeting', he was described to Quarter Sessions in 1684 as follows: 'Thomas Meddlicott, of Cheshunt, formerly one of Oliver Cromwell's own troop, a great and constant companion of Rombald's who hath been an holder-forth at Hackney amongst the Anabaptists, never was at his parish church that any can tell of this twenty years, a great ring-leader and lawgiver amongst all the phanaticks, one that hath paid his debts by swearing himself not worth £10 though he lives plentifully; by which he cheated a Scotch gentleman of £500 and would not pay him so much as one penny to bear his charges back again to Scotland, as Hardinge, the constable of Cheshunt, can witness. When he was sent for to the sessions at Waltham Cross he professed himself to be a Seeker, and that there is no church in the world pure enough for him to communicate withal. If he be not made to comply with the church the rest of the phanaticks will never be brought to any compliance. He was chosen churchwarden by the parish but would never execute any of the justices' warrants'. From this description and the fact that he was not listed as a Baptist in 1682, it seems reasonable to guess that Medlicot *may* have become a Ranter or Seeker, an extreme seventeenth century sect. Perhaps the other nine people listed with him in 1682 were also Seekers. One of them was John Cordle, cow leech.[19] Was he related to William Cordle of Cheshunt in whose house there had been massive drinking during St Giles' Fair in 1598 (see page 14)?

While the Cheshunt Baptists carried on a living tradition from Cromwellian times, the PRESBYTERIANS and INDEPENDENTS, who seem to have worshipped together, not only had links with the past but were to be involved in the future with the 1688 settlement. Among the early spiritual leaders of this congregation was John Yates, the vicar of Cheshunt from 1656 to 1660 who was ejected on the

Restoration of Charles II but seems to have continued living locally. He died in 1679 and, according to Calamy, was then 'near an hundred years of age'.[20] Anthony Palmer, a London pastor, was preaching 'at a house in Theobalds Park' in 1665 when 'Sir Henry Wroth, of Durants [in Middlesex] . . . came with a body of soldiers'. Palmer fortunately escaped. In 1669 the Hertfordshire JPs ordered the constables to disperse the 'unlawful assemblies of great numbers of persons' which took place frequently at Theobalds and at houses called the King's Stables. If the assemblies refused to disperse the principals who taught or preached were to be arrested. Robert Bragge and Thomas Wadsworth were named as the Theobalds preachers in this year. Thomas Wadsworth died in 1676 aged forty-six; Robert Bragge preached his funeral sermon. Bragge lived until 1704; he was seventy-five when he died and, by then, minister of a Congregational church in London. On 1 May 1672 Thomas Wadsworth had been licensed as a Presbyterian teacher and John Yates as a Congregational teacher, both in Jonathan Pritman's house which was licensed as a Presbyterian meeting-place. There was a separate, licensed Congregational meeting-place at Thomas Pothill's house, at which Christopher Fowler was licensed as a Congregational teacher. Christopher Fowler died in 1679 in Southwark. Urwick also mentions Abraham Hume who 'preached privately at Theobalds and there continued till King James's liberty'.

The Sessions Records [Vol I, pp 324-5] contain a fascinating list of sixty-nine 'names of some of the wealthiest Dissenters in the parish of Cheshunt'. The 1676 Compton Return, incidentally, recorded sixty-three Dissenters in Cheshunt. In the 1682 list there were six 'such as are Anabaptists', eleven Quakers, and ten 'such as seldom go to church'. The overwhelming majority, forty-two were 'such as joyne with the Presbyterians and Independents at the meeting in Theobalds'. The list contains the names of important people, some with London connections. While the Quaker tentacles reached from market towns into villages in the county, the Theobalds' congregation seems to have been linked to the capital. The three 'Teachers' were Mr Robert Bragge, 'Mr Castair a Scott' and Mr Samuel Otway. John Stockin was 'their clerk at the meeting'. William Barefoot was the 'schoolmaster, excommunicated formerly and indicted at the sessions'. In 1677 he had been presented because he 'kept a school and was a schoolmaster, outside any university or college of the Kingdom, and in no public or free grammar school, nor in the service of any "noble man or noble woman" or gentleman or gentlewoman not being recusants and not licenced by the Diocese of Lincoln'. He was presented and indicted in 1682 for the same offence, keeping a grammar school without licence. In 1677 Barefoote was described as a yeoman but in 1682 as a clerk, that is a cleric. Bragge, Carstairs and

Otway were, actually, described as labourers in a presentment in 1682.

William Carstairs or Carstares is particularly interesting; he was William of Orange's chaplain during the 1688 invasion. As royal chaplain, with much influence over William III, he was nicknamed 'the Cardinal'. Between 1672 and 1683 or 1684, he was in Scotland and England, in and out of prison, involved in the Rye House 'plot', and tortured. Had his presence in Cheshunt in 1682 anything to do with the Rye House plot? The first name on the list of lay members was the Sheriff of Middlesex, Samuel Shute; 'Mrs Mary Shute, relict of Mr Benjamin Shute' was the fifth name. Benjamin Shute, a London merchant, was the father of John Shute, who became the first Viscount Barrington; John had been born at Theobalds in 1678. 'Mr Robert De Luna who entertains Castair in his house' followed Shute. As Robert Delluna esquire he was presented for not having received 'the blessed Sacrament of the Lord's Supper' in Cheshunt church for a whole year. However a certificate was produced to the effect that he was 'one of the members of the French Church, London, and doth receive the sacrament'. Presumably this was the Huguenot Church. On 9 March 1683 a further certificate explained that he was a French merchant who had left his country house at Cheshunt to live in Hackney. Isaac Eure, barrister-at-law, followed De Luna. Mr Thomas Abney followed Eure and preceded Mary Shute. Abney was a 'London citizen and fishmonger', born in 1640; 'in early life he cast his lot with the nonconformists, and joined the church in Silver Street under the care of Dr Jacomb'. William III knighted him. He was Lord Mayor of London in 1700-1, an MP 1701-2, and President of St Thomas' Hospital for many years. He had a 'summer retreat at Theobalds' where he died in 1722.[21] After these five names there appears the entry 'All these have their families all summer in Cheshunt but never come to their parish church, but do all they can to encourage the meeters'.

Two families are named further down the list: 'Dr James Desborough, MD, and all his family'; and 'Mr John Drew, an attorney and his wife and family'. Dr James Desborough was the nephew of Major-General John Desborough who had married Oliver Cromwell's sister. It is worth remembering that Richard, Oliver's son and successor, came to live in Cheshunt about 1683 with the Pengelly family, using the name John Clarke. Most of the remaining names are, probably, of local people, for example 'Robert Rolfe, baker', 'Hester, wife of John Ward, butcher', and 'William Tuttey, baker'. There were six widows in the list. The most interesting two local people are 'Mr John Graye, now churchwarden' and 'John Sole, constable, who hath lately come to his parish church once in a day but his wife scarcely ever'. Since two years after this list was compiled, Thomas Medlicot was described as 'chosen churchwarden by the parish', it would seem that the Dissenters successfully controlled the Vestry in Cheshunt. Mr John Gray was regularly picked on by the JPs, in the 1680s, for not receiving the sacrament, ironic for a churchwarden. In 1687 John Gray of Cheshunt gentleman was presented to Quarter Sessions for creating a nuisance by 'turning the offals in his mansion house . . . in Cheshunt through several yards belonging to' his neighbours. John Sole was constable as early as 1672 when a local butcher, Edward Lawrence, assaulted him. In April 1682 he was 'suppressed from keeping an alehouse in Cheshunt, as he does not attend his Parish Church, or any other church or chapel'. In July 'having brought a certificate that he goes to church' he was given 'liberty to draw bear as heretofore'. However on 29 September he was accused of selling drink on Sundays.

Whatever Dame Anne Sadleir may have hoped and the Cavalier Parliament sought to achieve, 'the vulgar people' had not been restored 'to their former obedience'. The simple courage of John Parsons, content to 'go to gaol for not working on Sundays', was as much an expression of independence among ordinary people as Richard Rumbold's dramatic words on the scaffold in 1685: 'I am sure there was no man born marked of God above another; for none comes into the world with a saddle on his back, neither any booted and spurred to ride him'.[22] The independence of men 'all alike in power', as the Thundridge shoemaker had put it in 1660, expressed itself openly in the 1680s both in social and economic actions and in expressions of political opinion. This was the local background to the national upheavals in the decade 1678 to 1688 of which the dramatic events described in the next chapter were a part.

Local contempt for authority

The two volumes of Hertfordshire Sessions records which cover the second half of the seventeenth century are a mine of information about popular attitudes to authority. There was simple drunken misbehaviour, such as that in Tudor and early Stuart times, which now began to express itself in open contempt for JPs. There were more outbursts of political opinion. The two merge into one another but for convenience can be described separately.

ALEHOUSE DISORDERS, like Edward Humerstone of Amwell's 'keeping a disorderly house' in 1675, were nothing new. He kept 'such company as . . ., drinking, revelling, singing and roaring on Sabbath days all day, yea even in sermon time'. Equally familiar was Stephen Barrow of Broxbourne's willingness, in 1683, to let gentlemen's servants pass their time in tippling 'to the loss of their time . . . and the hindrance of their masters' business'. There was a new element in John Searle alias Savill's behaviour in the White Hart at Ware in 1684. Three witnesses, one a bricklayer, another a fisherman, gave evidence that on 31 March about 8 or 9 o'clock in the evening Searle had used 'several abuses and ill language' against Sir Thomas Byde, who had been MP for Hertford Borough, and Skinner Byde, JP. The White Hart landlord in 1684 was Joseph Benson. Is it entirely a coincidence that in 1689 the White Hart at Ware was licensed by Joseph Parker, its then owner, as a Dissenters' Meeting House?

A more subtle piece of social impertinence by Joseph Bangham, a dyer, took place in the White Lion, Bishops Stortford in the evening of 13 April 1686. We have a detailed account of what happened. Bangham was drinking with two Londoners, a butcher and a ship's carpenter, and two fellow Stortford residents, Edward Johnson a tailor and Edward Ashby a draper. They were 'drinking and sometimes singing till about ten o'clock at night', when a JP who lived opposite, John Yardley, 'Dr in Physick', sent for Ashby. When he got up to go, Bangham said 'A plague of God rot him, don't go; you are a fool if you do', and 'I wish I were to go; if the justice had sent for me I would have gone, for I know well enough how to speak to a justice', adding 'By God, we come to be merry'. Then Yardley, the JP 'came over the way in person . . . and spoke to . . . Joseph Bangham as he sat alone on the bench behind the table'. Yardley 'told him twas time to go home, and that it was not fit to make such a noise at such a time of night to disturb the neighbours that they could not sleep . . . Joseph Bangham . . . just stirred his hat and clapped it on again, sitting on his tail and replied to the justice he would go home when he had made an end of his drink'. In appearance this was an ordinary drunken outburst but one witness, Anne Allmond, stated that she believed Bangham 'was not drunk when he spoke these words and committed this misbehaviour'. Another witness, Abraham Durrington of Bishops Stortford, blacksmith, added that after the JP left 'Bangham rose from the table and came to the rest of the company who were withdrawn from him to the fire's side, and said "Zounds what were you all fools to stand with your hats off to the justice. What, is he a king you see? I kept my hat on"'. In fact this has all the marks of a deliberate act of social defiance. The phrase 'sitting on his tail' is an illuminating echo of a phrase used by Sir Harbottle Grimston in his 'observations of the States Countreys': 'in their families they are all equals . . . Malkis [the maid servant] can prate as much, laugh as loud, and sit on her tail as well as her mistress'.[23] Refusing to doff one's hat was the contemporary Quaker form of protest against social and religious inequality.

Attacks on JPs, at least verbal ones, continued. In April 1688 Benaiah Aldin of Rickmansworth was bound over for 'very opprobrious and contemptuous words of Mr Fotherley and other His Majesty's Justices of the Peace'; and William Kidley of Barkway for 'very saucy and contemptuous words of this Court and of the Justices'. By this time there may have been an overt political-religious significance in these attacks on JPs, for James II had purged the JPs in many counties. John, son of Sir John Wittewronge of Rothamsted, wrote to his father from Buckinghamshire in March 1687: 'we had at our Assizes a Popish sermon and Popish justices and all the rest put out'. James, Sir John's younger son, had written a year earlier, in June 1686: 'we hear my Lord Chancellor [the notorious Jeffrys] intends to visit us at Lincoln's Inn the next week, what he will do is not known, some say he will purge our Bench of all the Whigs and turn out our preacher, and all our names are returned to him in order to have a character of every one'.[24]

The JPs were not the only objects of local disrespect. Constables, although neighbours, were not always appreciated. In 1683 Edward Chapman of Standon was indicted for 'pulling off' a warrant from the hands of John Peirepoint, a Standon constable, and cancelling the same. In 1688 Thomas Hankin, constable of Rushden, had a warrant to serve on Charles Funerall who turned on him with 'why do you follow me with your pimping warrant?' To keep in with their neighbours some constables failed to carry out their legal obligations. In 1684 constables were reported to have refused to join with other officers in presenting Dissenters. One case concerned Hemel Hempstead where the Compton Return of 1676 had reported one-fifth of the population were Dissenters. 'There is a Quakers' meeting constantly held every Sunday at Wood Green, in Hemel Hempstead parish. Mr Marston, one of the high constables of Dacorum Hundred lives hard by and I don't hear he ever disturbed them'.

No doubt disrespect for authority was endemic; it seems to have increased in the 1680s; certainly it was more openly expressed and alarmed those in power. When the county's JPs published a new table of 'Servants Wages' in April 1687, they made very clear their attitude to their social inferiors. 'Servants' were not just domestic servants, but also 'servants of husbandry', that is 'labourers' and craftsmen. The JPs fixed the most severe punishments for conspiring 'together to advance the prices of their work or wages', and in a preamble explained why: 'the licentious humours of some servants have prevailed so far upon the lenity and good nature of their masters, that they have advanced the charge of their wages and the expence of their diet above the rents of their masters' farms . . . their unreasonable and unlawful doings are become the general complaint of the inhabitants of this County'.

Open contempt for authority in more and more cases took on POLITICAL forms. The 1683 sessions had to deal with Daniel Gates, a Layston gentleman accused of holding an unlawful conventicle in his barn. On 1 October he was indicted for speaking dangerous and seditious words against the king and the government, which were 'That the high constable that made the warrants (by virtue of which the

petty constable of Layston went and disturbed the conventicle . .)
was a blockhead; and when it was told him that it was by order of the
justices of the peace, [he] replied that he had known justices of the
peace hanged, and that he hoped to see a gallows in Buntingford
street, and that he did not doubt but to see three or four score thousand hanged, and their throats cut before we should have good days;
and further, that if God Almighty be just he will rain fire and brim-
stone on the heads of the justices who disturbed the conventicle.
And there being discourse between the said Daniel Gates and some
persons concerning the late plot against His Majesty and the Duke of
York, he said he did not believe there was any plot.' The two Layston
constables, an esquire and a gentleman, as well as a local locksmith
and a grocer, were called upon to give evidence against Gates. The
plot referred to was, of course, the Rye House plot.[25] The Rye House
in Hoddesdon belonged to Richard Rumbold who was deeply
involved in the supposed assassination scheme. Rumbold had local
support. At the July 1683 sessions the JPs ordered the arrest of John
Leonard of Broxbourne 'for speaking dangerous words in the vindi-
cation of Richard Rumbold, who is mentioned in the king's proclamation for conspiring the death of the king and the Duke of York'. 'After
the king's messenger had been to apprehend [Rumbold] of treason',
Leonard was accused of 'saying that Rumbold was an honest man,
and that if he was there he would beat them all out of the room'. One
of the accusations against Thomas Medlicot in 1684 was that he had
been 'a great and constant companion of Rombald's'.

At the 1685 sessions there were two reported cases of political disaffection. John Lesteridge of Ware was charged with being disaffected against the government. John Thorpe, an Essendon labourer, was
accused of speaking several 'dangerous' words; they turned out to be
that 'he wished that they were hanged that first made the Act of
Parliament for the hearth money'; these were regarded by the authorities as malicious and opprobious words concerning the king. The
authorities soon had more serious matters to deal with than criticism
of the tax system. The Duke of Monmouth's landing on 11 June 1685
produced something like panic in the Hertfordshire authorities. On
17 and 18 June the constables of Ware were ordered to bring before
the JPs, on 22 June, twenty named 'persons of the said town dissent-
ing from the the present government, who may be dangerous, especially in this time of the rebellion of the Duke of Monmouth'. They
were to be brought to the George in Ware. Similar orders, to bring
three people to the Glove and Dolphin in Hertford, went to the constables of Hertingfordbury, to the constables of Bramfield for two
people, and to those of Bengeo for one person. Monmouth was
defeated on 6 July and captured on 8 July. On 7 July the Earl of
Middleton, who was James II's Secretary of State, wrote to the Lord

Lieutenant of Hertfordshire, the Earl of Bridgewater, telling him that the rebels had been defeated and adding 'that to prevent the escape of such of the rebels, as are not yet taken, . . . His Majesty would have you . . take all possible care, by . . . apprehending . . . all persons . . . who shall be found travelling up and down, and are not very well known, and also for searching all suspicious places and houses for any of the rebels or their abettors'. Bridgewater sent copies of this letter to the County's JPs on the next day, 8 July. On the back are rough notes of people bound over for saying that 'the Duke of Monmouth was upon his march with four-score thousand men'.

At the midsummer 1685 sessions the JPs discharged seventeen people who had been committed as disaffected persons, because they gave good sureties to keep His Majesty's peace and be of good behaviour, but committed nine more. The odd thing is that only one of these twenty-six people was among the twenty-six summoned for 22 June; this was Mr William Collett of Ware. Quarter Sessions were concerned with more than these fifty-one people; there is, for example, a list of people from Little Berkhamsted who were bound over in sums of £50 and £100, considerable amounts of money in those days. Among the seventeen discharged were William Collett and Gabriel Barber, doctor in physic, who had a name familiar from the Civil War. His namesake, probably his father, had been a leading figure on the committees which organised Hertfordshire for war in support of Parliament. Seven of the nine people who were committed were Dissenters, five of them the Baldock Quakers whose persistent law breaking has already been described. The other two were Richard Thomas and Thomas Grubb. Richard Thomas, a Hertford brewer, was described as a person formerly in arms against King Charles I. In 1662 he had been in trouble for not attending his parish church and refusing to take the oath of allegiance. In 1664 he had attended a conventicle. Thomas Grubb of Hertingfordbury was described as a disaffected person who refused to go to church. He had been presented for this offence as early as 1671 but, in spite of this, was chosen as chief constable for Hertford Hundred in 1678, continuing in office until 1680. These were, of course, the years in which the Whigs controlled the central government.

The other two who were committed were more purely political offenders. Owen Love's offence was inciting people to rise for the late Duke of Monmouth; Monmouth had been executed on 15 July. While Charles Etheridge was described as a person disaffected to the government, formerly a preacher at conventicles, there may have been a good deal more to it than that. John Etheridge, a Stortford baker and very likely a relative, came before this same midsummer 1685 Quarter Sessions for saying 'that where the king had one on his side, the Duke of Monmouth had thirty, and where the said king's health was drunk once, the said Duke's was drunk ten times'. A fascinating insight into the activities of Monmouth's supporters came in a quite separate piece of evidence from Thomas Wells who claimed that 'William Norman and John Mills with two others came over to him and asked him to play football, but that was not the business: 'twas to go and be listed for the Duke of Monmouth'.

The JPs then moved higher up the social scale. On 13 July they ordered that Sir John Read, Colonel Titus, William Field of Offley and Nicholas Martin of Hoddesdon be apprehended 'as suspicious people against the Government'. These were much bigger fish than the Quakers and the Dissenters. Sir John Read had been Sheriff in 1655, 1671, 1673 and 1676. He or a son was to be Sheriff again in 1693. Colonel Silius Titus of Bushey was one of the most notorious turncoats of the seventeenth century. He took up arms for Parliament in the Civil War, became an active royalist in the late 1640s, and is supposed to have been, at least partly, responsible for the text of 'Killing NO Murder'. This was written to justify the execution of Charles I but published to justify assassinating Oliver Cromwell! Titus was a virulent opponent of the regicides in the Restoration parliament, but in 1678-9 he became MP for Hertfordshire as the popular candidate of the 'Country Party' Whigs. In the parliaments of 1678-81 he forcibly opposed the succession of a Roman Catholic, the future James II, producing the lines:

'I hear a lion in the lobby roar,
Say, Mr Speaker, shall we shut the door?
Or do you rather choose to let him in?
But how then shall we get him out again?'

After 1681 Titus kept a low profile but it was not unreasonable to assume that such a weathercock might have supported Monmouth in 1685. In actual fact he joined James II's privy council in July 1688; as Macaulay put it with acid wit he 'had laboured to unite the Puritans with the Jesuits in a league against the constitution'.[26] Needless to say Titus returned to parliament in 1690 having made his peace with William III. Titus' behaviour in 1688 was in line with that of James, fourth Earl of Salisbury, except that Titus was more sure footed. For three generations the Cecils had been cautious parliamentary and Whig supporters. In 1688 James became a Roman Catholic and was promptly rewarded with public offices. His fate was described as follows: 'This earl had the ill-luck to turn papist just two or three months before the Prince of Orange came in, and became a mighty fat unwieldy man so that he could scarce stir with ease, though he was not over thirty-nine or forty years old. . . When he heard that the prince was landed he lamented sadly and curst and damned all about him, crying "Oh God, Oh God, I turn'd too soon, I turn'd too soon".'[27]

Less than three and a half years after Monmouth's landing, William of Orange had landed at Brixham, near Torbay, invited by the very same gentry and peers who had abandoned Monmouth and supported James II in 1685. William landed on 5 November, with much the same public aims as Monmouth's though without the radical overtones. James II's army joined William and James II fled. On 18 December 1688 William reached St James; he summoned a parliament which declared him and his wife, James II's daughter, joint sovereigns as William III and Mary II; this was on 13 February 1689. The Protestant succession was assured; Roman Catholics were excluded from the throne; and an Act of Toleration allowed men and women to worship how they pleased. The 'Glorious Revolution' was glorious because it was peaceful, and peaceful because an otherwise divided 'establishment' was temporarily united in inviting William of Orange. There was no civil war, no rebellion of the people such as had been threatened in 1685. Anglican Tories believing in the absolute right of succession of the hereditary monarch for a moment united with Whigs who sympathised with Dissenters and wanted a constitutional monarchy.

NOTES

1   Christopher Hill *The World Turned Upside Down*. Penguin 1975.

2   Inscription in the Trinity College *Apocalypse*. Trinity College Mss. R.16.2.

3   *Report on the Manuscripts of the Earl of Verulam*. HMC. 1906, pp 225-6. The original Ms [HCRO. Gorhambury IX.A.6a] is signed 'Harb. Grimeston'. There is a fascinating puzzle as to the author. A very similar text was printed in 1652 and reprinted in 1660 'for Henry Seile' who claimed that 'the Author . . . long since traveling for companies-sake with a friend' had 'his puerilia' pirated. So Seile 'having a perfect copy by me' published it. This text is attributed in the Cambridge University catalogue to Owen Feltham [Peterborough H.3.25 and U^X.8.70(G)]. I have not discovered why. The Seile text has many additional passages but also, as compared with the Grimston one, some obvious errors: 'tread' for 'spread' and 'fat' for 'flat'. Most interestingly, in the passages which I have quoted, 'as we choose aldermen' in the Seile text is rendered 'as our kings choose sheriffs for the counties'; and 'Malkis' is 'Malky' and 'on her tail' is omitted.

4   *Cobbett's Complete Collections of State Trials* Vol. V. 1810, pp 1287 & 1289; taken from *The Speeches and Prayers of Major General Harison . . . Daniel Axtell*. 1660, pp 82 & 84. The texts are identical but capitalisation different.

5   *Hertford County Records* Vol I *Notes and Extracts from the Sessions Rolls 1581-1698* compiled by W J Hardy. 1905, p 131. Where no other reference is given in this chapter quotations come from this volume or Vol VI *Calendar to the Sessions Books . . . and other Sessions Records 1658-1700,* William Le Hardy. 1930.

6   Quoted in Sir Charles Firth *Oliver Cromwell* (1901). 1933 reprint, p 367.

7   HCRO D/ELW F29.

8   William Urwick *Nonconformity in Herts.* (1884), p 542.

9   The statistics of the Compton Return for Hertfordshire are from Lionel Munby *Hertfordshire Population Statistics 1563-1801.* Hertfordshire Local History Council (1964).

10 *The Journal of George Fox,* revised edition by John L Nickalls. (1952). pp 228-9 and 520.

11 Joseph Besse *A collection of the Sufferings of the People called Quakers.* (London 1753), Vol I pp 241-2. All quotations, unless otherwise indicated, are from Besse pp 248-54 or the Hertford County Records – see Note 5.

12 William Urwick *Nonconformity in Herts.* (1884), p 506. Urwick and Besse print King, W J Hardy and William Le Hardy sometimes King, sometimes Ring. Capital K and R can be confused. I stick to King.

13 *Ibid.* p 507

14 *Ibid.* p 537

15 *Oxford English Dictionary.*

16 Urwick *op. cit.* p 507

17 *Ibid.* p 508

18 *Ibid.* p 559

19 Sessions Rolls *op. cit.* Vol I, pp 348 & 324-5.

20 Urwick *op. cit.* pp 505-6 & 509. All the quotations which follow concerning Theobalds, not from the Sessions Rolls, are from Urwick pp 509-12.

21 *DNB* Vol I, pp 54-5.

22 *State Trials* XI (1811), p 881

23 Mss of the Earl of Verulam *op. cit.*

24 HCRO D/ELW F28 & F29.

25 Peter Rich, the sheriff of Hertfordshire, wrote to Sir Leoline
    Jenkins, Secretary of State, on 13 July 1683 that 'this Daniel
    Gates is a most desperate, violent person and I cannot the least
    doubt he is in the conspiracy'. He enclosed a report dated the
    day before that 'Daniel Gates, alias Yates, now in our county gaol
    for want of sureties for his good behaviour, has lying in his yard .
    . . a considerable number of cannon shot, some of them crossbar
    shot'. [*Calendar of State Papers Domestic* July 1 to September 30
    1683, pp 104 & 109].

26 *The Works of Lord Macaulay. History of England* Vol III. Longmans
    (1898) p 194.

27 Quoted without reference in *Hertfordshire Families* edit by
    Duncan Warrand (*VCH*), p 120, where the remark is attributed to
    Prynne. William Prynne, the Puritan pamphleteer whose style it
    might seem to be in, died in 1669!

PART TWO

THE RYE HOUSE PLOT 1683

~3~
PROTESTANT PLOT OR POPISH CONSPIRACY
1683-89

On the morning of Friday 13 July 1683 the body of Arthur Capel, Earl of Essex, of Much Hadham and of Cassiobury in Watford was found in his room in the Tower of London with his throat 'cut from the one jugular to the other'.[1] Three days earlier, on Tuesday 10 July, Sir Leoline Jenkins, Secretary of State, had committed the Earl of Essex to the keeping of Thomas Cheek, lieutenant of the Tower, 'for high-treason in compassing the death of the king and conspiring to levy war against his majesty'. On the same day as Capel died William Lord Russell, son of the Earl later the Duke of Bedford, was tried and found guilty of high treason. The jury's decision was influenced by Essex's supposed suicide. This was very convenient for Charles II and his brother, James Duke of York, for it seemed to be an admission of guilt and so to prove the existence of a Protestant Plot against the Crown. Treason trials had begun on 12 July 1683. Among those indicted 'for high treason, in conspiring the death of the king and the duke of York, subversion of the government, etc', and who were later executed, was Richard Rumbold of the Rye House, Hoddesdon, which gave its name to the supposed plot.[2] The fate of these two

Plate 4 The Rye House. Print after a drawing by H. Edridge, published 1824. [British Museum].

Hertfordshire people, the peer and the commoner, is worth investigating in its own right, for their stories are dramatic, but they also reveal much about the conflicts of the later years of Charles II's reign.

There was in seventeenth century England a deep seated paranoia about Roman Catholics which was intensified by Charles II's pro-French policies and influenced by his brother, James Duke of York's, conversion. Between 1678 and 1681 this paranoia erupted in the Popish Plot hysteria. Titus Oates, a plausible rogue, and many imitators produced accusations of Roman Catholic plans to seat James on the throne. For three years Charles II had to bow to well orchestrated pressure from the Earl of Shaftesbury's newly formed Whig party. In 1679 the Earl of Essex became First Lord of the Treasury in what amounted to a Whig government forced on Charles II. When Charles II regained control in 1681 he began systematically undermining the basis of Whig support in the country. By 1682 this had developed into an all out attack on the Whig leaders. The supposed Protestant plot of 1683 was the culmination of the Court's counter attack. David Ogg compared the consequences of the two plots, a little one-sidedly: 'The Popish Plot had destroyed about a score of persons, mainly priests or Jesuits; the Stuart revenge, on the other hand, had removed some of the most distinguished representatives of the English aristocracy'.[3]

There is an equally significant comparison to be made. Almost all historians accept that the informers' tales of Popish plots were fictitious and that innocent people died because of them. The interpretations of the Protestant plot are very different. Lord Macaulay in the 1840s wrote that 'unscrupulous and hot-headed chiefs of the [Whig] party proposed that there should be simultaneous insurrections in London, in Cheshire, at Bristol, and at Newcastle. Communications were opened with Scotland; a design of a very different kind was meditated by some of their accomplices, to waylay and murder the king and his brother. A place and a time were named; and the details of the butchery were frequently discussed if not definitely arranged. Both plots were soon discovered. Cowardly traitors hastened to save themselves, by divulging all, and more than all.' Many, but not all, later historians have accepted that this was a real plot, in two parts, 'the said design against the king and the duke [of York], as also of a general insurrection, which they distinguished by the names of the Lopping Point, and General Point'. Some writers have believed in one, some in the other part of the plot. Recent specialist studies seem to have been less sceptical than those publishing between 1934 and 1977.[4] This is not the place to reopen the debate. My purpose is more limited, simply to explore the degree of guilt of Richard Rumbold, accused of being the would be assassin at the centre of plans for the 'Lopping Point', and to ask whether the Earl of Essex really committed suicide or was, in fact, murdered.

Richard Rumbold and the Lopping Point

The Earl of Shaftesbury, as he became more afraid of the King's revenge in 1682, began plotting resistance. He claimed that he had the support of 10,000 brisk boys. They were organised in clubs centred on taverns. Members were sworn to secrecy. There must have been times when there was wild talk in such clubs. One can believe that old soldiers from Cromwellian times could, in their cups, have *discussed* innumerable mad schemes like those of which they were to be accused: seizing the Tower, overawing the royal guards, and assassinating the royal brothers. Such an atmosphere was an ideal breeding ground for government agents, agent-provocateurs. All the evidence that there was a real assassination plot in existence comes from men who turned king's evidence after others had accused them of involvement. Col. John Rumsey, whom several witnesses described as the link man between Shaftesbury and the lesser conspirators, heard at second hand that Robert West had described 'an intention to assassinate the king, at his coming from Newmarket in October . . . though it miscarried at that time it was not to be given over'. Robert West, who became the chief government informer, described how 'Mr Richard Rumbold and a party of his friends designed and were prepared to have killed the king and duke of York in their journey to or from Newmarket but the king and duke went an unusual way through the forest that time'. G N Clark, who believed the murder plan was real, described the Rye House, Richard Rumbold's home, the site for the planned murder: a 'narrow road ran between high banks, where the king often passed on his way to the [Newmarket] race-meetings or home. To block the road and seize the king's person seemed feasible enough: the plan was made and the day was fixed'.[5]

Two men were supposed to have been particularly involved in schemes for assassination. They had both been in the parliamentary army during the Civil War. Captain Thomas Walcot, the first man to be tried and executed in 1683, was described by Roger L'Estrange, the Tory press licenser, as 'the most daring, dangerous villain in the whole gang, I dread the man'. The outstanding figure among the supposed plotters of the 'lopping point' was 'Colonel' Richard Rumbold. Proper examination of Rumbold's life and statements is, therefore, necessary. He had joined the parliamentary army when he was nineteen, at the beginning of the Civil War. He was one of the guards round the scaffold at Charles I's execution. He was one of eight privates who petitioned Fairfax in February 1649 to restore the Agitators in the army. He fought at Dunbar and Worcester. By June 1659 he was a cavalry lieutenant. After the Restoration of Charles II he married a maltster's widow and carried on the trade at the Rye House, near

Hoddesdon, the site of the supposed assassination plot. He was indicted for high treason on 12 July 1683 and subsequently outlawed. One hundred pounds had been offered for his arrest on 23 June. There was a vigorous hue and cry. The Sheriff of Hertfordshire was ordered to 'use your utmost endeavours to apprehend Richard Rumball, a maltster; he is a one-eyed man and was an officer in Cromwell's army. He appears to be a most dangerous and desperate villain in the evidence we have of a design against His Majesty's person'. Rumbold was spotted all over the place and innocent people were arrested. On 7 July Sir Leoline Jenkins wrote to Yorkshire: 'His Majesty longs to hear what the Rumball you were in pursuit of will prove and the more in that there is another taken up for that villain, now lying in Exeter gaol'. On 23 July the order was given that another Rumbold 'taken in Northants and brought to Newgate be no longer detained [he] being not the man he was taken for but Henry Hutchinson, a miller'! The real Rumbold escaped to Holland.[6] Walcot had already been caught, tried and executed.

What is the evidence that these ex-Cromwellian officers and others really planned to murder Charles II and his brother? Details of the plots, especially of the 'lopping point', came from Robert West, 'a seedy barrister' as Maurice Ashley described him, and from Col. John Rumsey who 'some time since taken, as is said, discovered very considerably; it is certain he was very familiar with the late Earl of Shaftesbury; Mr West also makes considerable discoveries and is said to have his pardon'. These two were the key informers. Several others described continuing arrangements for 'taking off His Majesty', being discussed in Col. Rumsey's house on 27 December 1682. The next date mentioned was 'about the month of February' 1683. Rumsey described meeting at 'Mr West's chamber, to consider how the design should be brought to effect, at the king's return from Newmarket. West and Goodenough did desire [Rumsey] would be acquainted with Richard Rumball, the man that would command the party that should take off the king and the duke'. A fire at Newmarket caused the royal party to leave unexpectedly early; so the supposed attempt never materialised. Rumsey claimed that in March it was decided 'that arms should be brought [*sic*] against the next journey to Newmarket in Autumn or any other opportunity, as at the playhouse or coming from Windsor to Hampton Court'. West reported talk of this 'about Easter', 8 April, 'but no resolution was ever taken'. Another report was that 'after the fire happened at Newmarket, [West], Col. Rumsey, Walcot, Ferguson, Rumbold and Richard Goodenough had met twice, and resolved to let making any attempt upon the king and duke alone'.[7]

There are several reasons for being sceptical about these superficially convincing accounts of assassination plans. West's 'no resolution was ever taken' and 'let making any attempt upon the king and duke alone' give a clue. There may have been much talk of 'attempts' but there is remarkably little real evidence of hard plans being carried out. One of the more obvious inconsistencies is the coincidence that the two dates supposedly chosen by the conspirators for an attempt to be made at the Rye House were those on which accidents led the royal party to change their travel plans. Since Rumbold was portrayed by all the informers as a ruthless and determined man, a good reason had to be given to explain why an assassination was never actually attempted. Suggesting plans had been made for these two occasions gave a plausible explanation.

The key question is how reliable were the informers, men who by their own admissions were themselves involved and bought their safety by informing. David Ogg wrote that Rumsey and West would 'appear, if Burnet is to be credited, to have decided on a novel plan. This was to come in voluntarily with a "concocted confession" which would not only save their lives, but might qualify them for employment in detective work against the numerous emissaries of Satan then flourishing in England. An alternative explanation (of which there is no proof) is that the Court prompted the "confession" in order to implicate the Whigs. The document drawn up by West is comparable in its wildness and inconsistencies with the stories of Oates.'[8] Robert West had approached the Earl of Rochester, offering to tell all on 22 June 1683. On 23 June he began a massive series of statements stretching over many weeks. An order was made for the arrest of Col. John Rumsey on 23 June; £100 reward was offered. Rumsey was caught and made his first statement on 25 June. On 26 June Charles II, in person, examined West and Rumsey. On 4 July West told Sir Leoline Jenkins: 'I will do anything in my power to save my life'. He asked to take the Sacrament 'to give that test of my sincerity' and, on 5 July, added: 'Were I capable of giving evidence against the great men, I think I should be more ready to do it than against any other'. On 9 July the Privy Council heard from Rumsey: 'I will never fail to acquaint [the King] of any thing I can remember that may help to make a full discovery of this plot, wherein it was my great misfortune to be a vile consulter, for which I am a true penitent'. West and Rumsey were kept in captivity from July 1683 to the summer of 1684, cringing and whinging and regularly pleading for better treatment. The Court played cat and mouse with them.[9]

There is an extraordinary letter of 2 August 1683 in the Privy Council records purporting to be from Richard Rumbold, then a fugitive, to West:

'When I consider what misery has fallen on our party by your evidence, I cannot think of you but with amazement and horror, as if you were born for the subversion of your country and ruin of the

Protestant religion but, when I reflect with what subtilty and artifice our enemies deluded you and with what reluctancy you were induced to accuse *the men you had solicited and stirred up* [my italics], I cannot but have charity for your frailty and compassion for your sufferings, but when I further observe how you have eluded our enemies' malice by eluding them with hearsay informations and hallooing them on Hone, Rouse and Walcot and by the concealing of some and the late naming of others you have given a great many brave men not only warning but opportunity to escape, I cannot sufficiently admire your conduct nor can I believe that any other could have saved himself and so many other worthy men with the loss of only three, two whereof were the most inconsiderable of our party, and Hone and Walcot may more justly charge their murders on Percival and Shepherd than on you, who were compelled to do as you did by necessity, whereof your kindness to Capt Blague is a demonstration, but they were villains in cold blood and on choice. The blood of Lord Russell cries for vengeance against Shephard, Howard and that villain Rumsey, who, I am convinced, has been the Duke of York's spy and trepan managed by the Duke of Beaufort, ever since he was the little lord's privado*, and any one not crackbrained might have long since perceived it, had he been in that lord's station. I must entreat you not to abandon yourself to excessive sorrow, for the charity of your party is not to be despaired of. It is not unknown to any of us with what zeal and sincerity you led us on, whilst there were any hopes of succeeding, and I shall always represent you to our friends according to your merits and, now that you have put yourself out of the reach of your enemies by obtaining a pardon, I shall make it my sole business to set you right with your friends, to whom I owe my life, for, had not your wisdom directed me, Keeling's villainy had destroyed me.'[10]

If this was not a fake, it arouses innumerable speculations. Had West a pardon by August 1683? If so why was he kept in close custody till 1684? Was Rumsey really the Duke of York's spy? It is difficult to believe Rumbold could have thought so well of West.

The confessions of those who died for their part in the plot are revealingly specific and supportive of the view that the Rye House plot proper was a figment of the imagination of Rumsey and West. James Holloway who was executed on 30 April 1684 and Richard Nelthorp executed on 30 October 1685 both admitted that they knew

---

* Trepan *OED* = 'A person who entraps or decoys others into actions or positions which may be to his advantage and to their ruin or loss'; Privado = 'An intimate private friend, a confidant; the favourite of a ruler'.

and approved of early plans for insurrection. Holloway thought 'insurrection [was only] to get the king off from his evil council, and bring all popish offenders to justice'. They both denied any involvement in assassination plans. 'I never had any design against his majesty's person', said Holloway, but he had heard talk. It was to be 'carried on by Rumsey and West. I never heard of above five for it; it was carried on contrary to the knowledge or approbation of those who managed the general design'. Nelthrop's speech from the scaffold was even more specifically an implicit condemnation of the plot evidence. 'As to the design of assassinating the late king, or his present majesty, it always was a thing highly against my judgment, and which I always detested; and I was never in the least concerned in it, neither in the purse nor person, nor never knew of any arms brought for that intent, *nor did I believe there was any such design, or ever hear of any disappointment in such an affair, or time, or place, save what after the discovery of the general design, Mr West spoke of*, as to arms bought by him.' [my italics]. Bishop Burnet's comment on what Holloway said was damning. 'The credit of the Rye Plot received a great blow by his confession.' The plot 'had gone no further, than that a company of seditious and inconsiderable persons were framing among themselves some treasonable schemes, that were never likely to come to anything; and that Rumsey and West had pushed on the execrable design of the assassination'.[11]

West's accusations against Walcot were not so different from Walcot's own confession in gaol and on the scaffold. West claimed that as for the 'design upon the king and duke, as they came from Newmarket in October last [Walcot] told me he abhorred any such thing, and he would not be concerned in it, but only in general insurrection'. He 'refused a long time to act in any wise in the attempt upon the king and duke but at length by the persuasion of Ferguson he undertook to command the party who were to fight the guards but refused to act in the assassination itself'. At Walcot's trial Rumsey gave similar evidence. This was denied by Walcot who told the Newgate chaplain that 'he never made any promise to charge on the King's guards, because, if they had fallen, his Majesty had been left naked of defence, which in effect would have amounted to the crime of violating his person, which never entered into his thought'. During his trial on 12 July and on the scaffold on 20 July Walcot was quite specific: 'the death of the king' did not 'enter into my thoughts either directly or indirectly'. 'I was not for contriving the death of the king.' However he did admit that 'it was proposed when [he was present]. I do not know how far it was agreed. There were several meetings, wherein the business of the king's life was never spoke of; they were for asserting our liberties and properties; we were under general apprehensions, and so were those lords that are likely to suffer, under general apprehensions of popery and slavery coming in.'

On the scaffold Walcot was interrogated by Dr Thomas Cartwright, Dean of Ripon, who later actively supported James II's attacks on the Anglican church. When Cartwright poured scorn on Walcot's blaming those who had betrayed him, Walcot answered: 'these men, they did not come in against me, till they did it to save themselves. I cannot tell how to excuse my witnesses for aggravating things against me, and making them worse than they really were; for a man to invite a man to a meeting, to importune him to this meeting, to be perpetually soliciting him; and then deliver him up to be hanged, as they have done me'. At this point Dr Cartwright interrupted and silenced Walcot. Walcot was describing the way agents provocateurs worked; he might have named them; and there were many more trials and executions to come. Could the government have persisted if their witnesses had been named and their behaviour had been so precisely and so publicly described?[12]

In May 1685 Rumbold returned from exile as colonel of horse under the Earl of Argyle, who invaded Scotland just before Monmouth's invasion of England. 'Covered with wounds and defending himself with uncommon exertions of strength and courage [Rumbold] was at last taken.' As an outlaw he was already under sentence of death by an English court. Scottish justices tried him for his part in the invasion. He was executed. In the justices' court, 'he owned it all, saving that part of having designed the king's death; he never, directly or indirectly, intended such a villany'. At the Market Cross in Edinburgh before his execution, Rumbold explained that 'it was ever my thoughts, that kingly government was the best of all, justly executed; I mean, such as by our ancient laws; that is a king, and a legal, free-chosen parliament. The king [and] the people being, as it were, contracted to one another. How absurd to maintain that though the one party breaketh all conditions, the other should be obliged to perform their part.' He continued, as a cavalry officer, with the immortal words: 'I am sure there was no man born marked of God above another; for none comes into the world with a saddle on his back, neither any booted and spurred to ride him'. He added, revealing that he was a seventeenth century man not a twentieth century equalitarian: 'not but that I am well satisfied, that God has wisely ordered different stations for men in the world'. A hierarchical society did not entitle those above to ride roughshod over those below.

Are 'deathbed' statements of those about to be executed to be trusted rather than the massive, repeated assertions of those who turned King's evidence? On the reader's judgement rests the decision as to whether there really was a Rye House plot, a lopping point, or whether this was a government frame-up. In deciding, Charles James Fox's view is not irrelevant: 'the asseverations of dying men have always had great influence upon those who do not push their ill opinion of mankind to the outrageous and unwarrantable length'. Rumbold's 'solemn denial of the project of assassination imputed to him in the affair of the Rye-house Plot, is in itself a fact of great importance; and Walcot, with his last breath, denied his own participation in any design to murder either Charles or James'. There is a reason why Charles II and the Duke of York may have been especially malevolent in their feelings for Walcot and Rumbold. They had both been guards round the scaffold at Charles I's execution and Sir Leoline Jenkins was reminded on 25 June 1683 by David Fitzgerald that Walcot had been suspected of having been the king's executioner but acquitted for want of proof.[13]

Suicide or murder most foul? Did the Earl of Essex commit suicide?

On the first night of his arrest the Earl of Essex lay at 'captain Cheek's, but the next day was removed to major Hawley's (then gentleman porter of the Tower) and the two warders, then placed upon his lordship, were Nathaniel Monday and Thomas Russel; one of these was to stand for two hours at my lord's chamber door, or in his chamber, and the other at the stair's foot; and thus by turns'. The only other person 'permitted to be with his lordship' was Paul Bomeny who had been his servant for three or four years. About nine o'clock on Friday 13th morning 'his lordship was found [by Paul Bomeny and Thomas Russel] with his throat cut'. An inquest was held the next day, Saturday, by Edward Farnham, coroner of the liberty of the Tower of London with a jury of twenty-three 'good and lawful men of the liberty', who found that the earl 'voluntarily and feloniously did cut his throat'.[14]

One informed contemporary had his doubts. Evelyn confided to his diary on the very day of Essex's death: 'that astonishing newes of the Earle of Essex having Cut his owne Throat was brought to us, having now ben but three dayes prisoner in the Tower, and this happening on the very day and instant that the Lord Russel was on his Trial, and had sentence of death: This accident exceedingly amaz'd me, my Lord of Essex being so well know[n] by me to be a person of so sober and religious a deportment, so well at his ease, so much obliged to the King. It is certaine the King and Duke were at the Tower, and pass'd by his Window about the same time this morning, when My Lord asking for a rasor he shut himselfe into a closet and perpetrated the horrid fact: It was wondred yet by some how it was possible he should do it, in the manner he was found; for the wound was so deepe and wide, as being cut through the Gullet, Wind-pipe, and both the jugulars, it reached to the very Vertebrae of the neck, so as the head held to it by a very little skin as it were, which tack'd it from being quite [off]: The gapping too of the rasor, and cutting his owne fingers, was a little strange; but more, that having passed the Jugulars he should have strength to proceede so farr, as an Executioner could hardly have don more with an axe, and *there were odd reflections upon it'* [my italics].[15]

The evidence given to the coroner's inquest was from four people: Paul Bomeny, Thomas Russel, one of the warders, Robert Sherwood and Robert Andrews, 'chirurgeons'. The surgeons described the wound of which Essex 'certainly died' in almost the same words as Evelyn: 'the throat of the Lord of Essex . . . was cut from the one jugular to the other, and through the wind-pipe and gullet, into the vertebres of the neck, both jugular veins being also quite divided'. The 'Informations' of the inquest witnesses explained that 'the earl of Essex called for a penknife to pare his nails, but the penknife not being ready at hand, his lordship desired a razor, which was delivered to him, with which razor his lordship retired into his closet, and locked himself in; but soon after the closet door was opened, and that lord there found with his throat cut'.[16]

The unanimity of almost all later historians, who accepted the contemporary Bishop Burnet's opinion that Essex did commit suicide, flies in the face of contemporary pamphlet literature. The main authors were Robert Ferguson, Colonel Danvers and Lawrence Braddon. Danvers' and Ferguson's accounts add little to the considerable material collected by Lawrence Braddon. This is described in several publications: *Essex's Innocency and Honor vindicated* of 1690, and *Bishop Burnet's late History charg'd with great Partiality and Misrepresentation* of 1725; but first revealed in Braddon's trial, with Hugh Speke, for 'suborning witnesses to prove the Earl of Essex was murdered by his keepers'. This took place in February 1684. Sir George Jeffrys, by this time Lord Chief Justice, presided; there were other judges. A report of the trial was printed in 1684. Braddon was fined £2000 and remained in prison until William III landed.[17]

Braddon was a barrister of the Middle Temple, apparently uninvolved in political or religious controversy until Essex's death. There was no apparent motive for his obsessive conviction that Essex had been murdered except the belief that the truth was being concealed by those in authority. Interrogated by the Privy Council in Charles II's presence on Friday 20 July 1683, he was asked: 'What made me engage in that matter? [There was] no connection with the family; it was my love to Truth and Justice first ingaged me in it'. This is what Braddon remembered of the opening of his interrogation; he commented that at this point he noticed the Duke of York's 'concerned countenance; [he] covered his face with his hand'. It was Braddon who was active in 1689 in putting evidence before the special committee of enquiry into Essex's death, which was set up by the House of Lords in the Convention Parliament on 5 February 1689. Braddon's own explanation of how he came to believe Essex had been murdered was that he learnt, almost by accident, of suspicious incidents at the Tower which took place at the time of the supposed suicide. Following up this evidence more and more corrobatory facts were discovered. Braddon's detective instincts were strengthened because the authorities tried so hard to suppress his evidence, to refute it and to suggest he was motivated by fanaticism. Burnet described Braddon as someone 'whom I had known for some years for an honest but enthusiastical man, [who] hearing of these stories, resolved to carry the matter as far as it would go, and he had picked up a great variety of little circumstances, all which laid together seemed to him so convincing, that he thought he was bound to prosecute the matter. I desired him to come no more near me, since he was so positive.' Enthusiast in the late seventeenth century meant fanatic.[18] Did the earl commit suicide or was he murdered? To answer the question we need to consider Essex's character, the medical evidence, and the evidence of witnesses, circumstantial and second hand in many cases.

Essex's character

Bishop Burnet had been trusted by the widowed Countess of Essex with 'all the messages that had past between her lord and her while he was in the Tower'. He claimed that 'Essex had got into an odd set of some strange principles: and in particular he thought, a man was the master of his own life; and seemed to approve of what his wife's great grandfather, the earl of Northumberland, did, who shot himself in the Tower, after he was arraigned.* He had also very black fits of the spleen.' One of the inquest jurymen told the Lords' Committee that he had accepted the suicide verdict because Major Hawley had told the inquest that Essex 'had often declared that any man might cut his own throat to avoid an infamous death'. Hawley denied saying this, but there is pretty clear evidence that Hawley lied on several occasions. Braddon claimed, why we will see, that Hawley 'was justly suspected as highly criminal in relation to' Essex's death. The Earl of Arran wrote to Sir Leoline Jenkins, Secretary of State, that he 'was much surprised at the news of the Earl of Essex making away with himself, but, since that was in his thoughts, I do not much wonder at the manner of it, for I and other persons of quality have heard him say, when Alderman Quin cut his throat with a razor, that he thought it was an easy kind of death'.[19]

On the other hand many people agreed with Evelyn that Essex was 'a person of so sober and religious deportment'. Sergeant Jeffrys, as

---

* Sir Henry Percy, 8th Earl, in 1585, arraigned for intrigues with Mary, Queen of Scots.

he then was, must have felt Essex's character argued against suicide. In summing up for the prosecution at the end of Lord Russell's trial, he said: 'if you will argue from such uncertain conjectures [as character], then all criminals will come off. Who should think that my lord of Essex should be guilty of such desperate things which had he not been conscious of he would scarcely have brought himself to that untimely end, to avoid the methods of public justice.'[20]

The medical evidence

The way Essex's throat was cut seems to me to make a verdict of suicide highly unlikely, even if the evidence from character can be taken either way. Evelyn's description follows precisely the evidence of two surgeons at the inquest. The Lords' Committee in 1689 was told by 'several judicious physicians and surgeons, who were great anatomists, that they would not positively say that it was impossible for my lord to cut his throat [in the way it was cut]. But they never saw any man's throat so cut, which was cut by himself.' Modern medical opinion seems to agree. It may be significant that the surgeon who assured Burnet that Essex had committed suicide apparently believed that the 'aspera arteria', the windpipe, had not been severed, but it had been. The only available description of the razor, found by Essex's body, makes it even more improbable. It was said to be a French razor with a 4¼ inch blade and no spill or tongue, from which it was argued by Braddon that it could hardly have cut the Earl's cravat in three places and made a wound three inches or more deep of the kind described by the surgeons. This medical evidence, at the very least, suggests that historians should have looked seriously, as they do not seem to have done, at the conflicting evidence of what happened on Friday 13 July.[21]

What happened on Friday 13 July? The evidence of witnesses

Evidence of what happened in Essex's rooms on Friday 13 July was given at the inquest the next day by Paul Bomeny, his servant, and Thomas Russel, one of his warders. At Braddon's trial in February 1684 Bomeny and Russel reappeared, joined by Major Hawley and John Lloyd, the sentinel 'at my lord's door'. In 1689 Hawley, Lloyd and Russel all gave evidence to the Lords' Committee; they were joined by Nathaniel Monday, 'my lord's other warder'. Bomeny did not appear. He was French, a catholic and in France. Braddon claimed that Sir Henry Capel had had an offer from Bomeny to 'come to London' and give evidence about Essex's death if he had the money for the journey. Sir Henry sent money, though Braddon advised him not to, but 'after that remittance, Sir Henry Capel never heard of either Bomeny or money remitted'. This makes Bomeny's evidence, like Major Hawley's, suspect. There were three key points in the evidence: when and how had Essex obtained the razor found by his body and assumed to have been used to cut his throat? How was the door into the close stool closet, where· Essex's body was found, opened? Had anyone been admitted into Essex's apartment between 8 and 9 o'clock on the morning of Friday 13 July, the day on which he died?[22]

The evidence about the razor was contradictory and Bomeny, whose evidence was fundamental, makes a poor impression. The coroner wrote down what he told the inquest which was that Essex had asked for a penknife to pare his nails on Friday 13th and been given a razor instead. When the coroner asked 'farther questions, Bomeny began extremely to hesitate, and desired that himself might write his own information'. He was allowed to retire into a room 'where several persons were ready prepared to assist him'. What Bomeny then wrote for the coroner was that he had given Essex a razor on Thursday 12th and a servant had brought a penknife late on the 13th. At Braddon's trial Bomeny made a revealing slip: on the 13th morning, 'I was turning to come down from the chamber, and I saw my lord walking in the room, and picking of his nails with the penknife'. Jeffrys 'How? With a pen-knife?' Bomeny 'No, with the razor that I gave him'. Russel's evidence, at the inquest and trial, was that it was on Friday 13th, a little while before Essex died, that Essex had asked for a penknife and been given a razor by Bomeny. In 1689 Monday, who had been on duty at Essex's door 'for two hours before Russel (that morning my lord died) came to relieve him', claimed that 'about seven . . . he then saw my lord have this razor in his hand'. These contradictions were quickly appreciated. The Privy Council records of 16 July contain an anonymous letter to Sir Henry Capel: 'On perusing the Coroner's inquest printed to-day about my Lord of Essex there are such material differences between the informations of Bomeny and Russell that it makes many people apprehend that, if that matter might suddenly be thoroughly sifted, it is probable a great deal of villainy might appear. If the steward would recollect what day he sent the penknife and the footman what day he delivered it to Bomeny, it would clear up Bomeny's deposition a little better to people's understanding, which is much obscured by confounding Friday morning with Thursday's business, for, as that deposition is penned, I cannot find my lord used either the razor or penknife after Thursday morning and then Russell is false, who fixes it on Friday; and Bomeny is short in giving an account how my lord came by the razor again on Friday, since he pared his nails with it on Thursday before the penknife came.'[23]

The second key point is how the door into the closet where Essex's body was found was opened. The letter to Sir Henry Capel continued: 'Besides, the shutting and opening the door and the manner of discovering my lord is so contradictory and very odd between them that it alone looks very suspicious. I could wish therefore some further inquiries may be made both to satisfy the public and vindicate the honour of that noble lord, for what is published seems not to be done with much care.' Bomeny stated that he had returned to the room, could not see Essex, and assumed he was in 'the close stool closet', the door of which was shut. In his first, oral statement he 'pushed the door a little open, where he did see his lord lying all at length on the ground in his blood, and the razor near him on the ground'. In his written statement: 'he took up the hangings, and looking through the chink, he saw blood, and part of the razor, whereupon he called the warder, Russel, and the said Russel pushed the door open, and there they saw my lord of Essex all along the floor, without a perriwig, and all full of blood, and the razor by him'. At Braddon's trial Bomeny told much the same story, adding that 'the chink of the door [was] between the door and the wall'. 'The door could not be opened easily. I think Russel pushed at the door but could not open it very far, because my lord's foot was against the door'. Russel agreed that he opened the door: '*I found the key was on the outside of the door* [my italics], and I opened the door'. This evidence he gave to the inquest and repeated at Braddon's trial. However sworn evidence was given to the House of Lords Committee in 1689 that Monday claimed 'that neither Bomeny nor Russel could open the door, but that he being much stronger pushing with all his might broke it open'. Two of Essex's servants, William Turner and Samuel Peck, who 'were some of the first who entered my lord's chamber after my lord's death was discovered to those out of the house, [told the committee] that my lord's body lay in the closet, but most part of his legs out of the closet, [and] have farther sworn, that they then observed the print of a bloody foot upon my lord's stocking, and by the print it appeared to be made by one who must be coming out of the closet after my lord was dead'.[24]

The third key point was whether anyone had been admitted to Essex's apartment between 8 and 9 in the morning on which he died. Russel stated at Braddon's trial that 'no body went up or down all the time, but Bomeney' and 'no body could pass backwards or forwards but I must see them'. Lloyd, the sentinel 'below at the street door' confirmed that 'nobody came in, all the while I stood there, that I know of'. Before the 1689 committee 'Monday and likewise Russel denied that any men were that morning let in to my lord'. Lloyd, however, changed his story and gave evidence on 22 January 1689 'that about half an hour after eight two men by permission of the said warder [Russel] entered the said lodging; when they came out, he can give no account; about nine o'clock he heard a struggling and a little time after heard a crying, My lord is dead'. Two other witnesses gave evidence that on separate occasions Lloyd had admitted this. One of them added that Lloyd said he had acted 'by special order of major Hawley'.[25]

That Essex had committed suicide was the verdict of the jury when an inquest was held the day after the earl was found dead. That the jury were honest is likely, but they were browbeaten and the inquest was hurried and conducted in an unseemly manner. Essex's body had been stripped and washed; the inquest jury were not able to see it as found. When one of them asked to see Essex's clothes, the coroner, 'hastily called into that next room, returning (in a passionate manner) told the jury, it was my lord's body and not his clothes they were to sit upon'. Apparently Essex's cravat was cut in several places; if the jury had seen this they might have found it difficult to believe he had cut this and his neck himself. The tidying up had been done 'by the command of Major Hawley'. When 'some of that jury desired that they might be adjourned, and notice given to my lord's family, Hawley prevents the adjournment by telling the coroner [that] the king had declared he would not rise from the [Privy] Council board until their inquisition was brought to him'. A Mr Colston, one of the jury, claimed 'that had they not been hurried they should have' come to another verdict. For this indiscretion he was fined, pilloried and imprisoned in the Kings-bench prison. Hawley seems to have been managing the inquest, quite improperly, and, it would appear, he lied persistently to conceal his responsibility. He even declared 'that he was not near the jury' though several jurymen swore in 1689 that he was present at the inquest and that he had suggested to the jury that the king was impatient for their verdict. This was not Hawley's only lie: he told the Lords' Committee that on the morning of Essex's death he 'went out of his house at five o'clock in the morning, and did not go nigh his own house till news of my lord's death was brought him by Monday the warder'. However Richard Nicholson, a Tower warder on duty that day, gave evidence that Hawley was at his own house at eight o'clock; and Mary Johnson, 'a labouring woman to Major Hawley designing to go upstairs met Major Hawley coming down, who told her my lord was dead'.[26]

What Braddon uncovered

If it had not been for Lawrence Braddon's indefatigable detective work, it *might* seem, on a charitable interpretation, that this confusion of evidence was due to human failings and not the product of a cover up. Braddon's argument has three distinguishable elements. There is what we may call, for want of a better word, gossip, convincing to some at the time but in fact almost all irrelevant. There is hard evidence, from two children, produced at the time and supported by other evidence in 1689 which positively suggests the involvement of someone or some people in Essex's death. There is the undoubted fact that the government took extreme measures to suppress evidence that murder might have been committed.

For gossip we have Braddon's accusation that Jeffrys, congratulated on his handling of Braddon's trial, answered when drunk 'that though he was well satisfied that the Earl of Essex was murdered, his business was to stifle it'. Much more was made of the suggestion that Essex's death, and even the manner of it, had been talked about at places as far apart as Frome and Tonbridge before he died. The frequency of such stories, which were common also during the Popish Plot, makes them difficult to credit even if it was likely that would-be murderers would have gossiped so widely that in Essex's case their intentions reached the ears of a pinmaker, a shopkeeper, and a stapler living fifty or more miles from London! One piece of evidence that murder had been planned is rather more credible; it was bitterly disputed in 1689 before the Lords' Committee. Dorothy Smith, 'servant with one Holmes, in Baldwin's Gardens', stated that 'about nine days before my lord's death she heard several papists discoursing concerning the taking off the earl of Essex. His highness [James Duke of York] had ordered his throat to be cut.' Six people gave evidence they had heard Dorothy Smith tell this story before 1688 and that 'she did hope to live to see the day, wherein she might fully testify without danger'. Dorothy Smith's evidence was challenged and Holmes' innocence defended by his sister Dorothy Hewit, 'a most violent papist', and Elizabeth Christopher, 'of a very loose character', as Braddon denigrated them. They swore that 'in April before Essex's death Dorothy Smith was turned away from Mr Holmes' upon suspicion of having stolen a silver spoon'. Six witnesses contradicted this evidence with picturesque detail: 'green-pease were very plenty and cheap' while she was in Holmes' service. Hewit then swore that she and Holmes were out of London between 6 and 23 July; and Nathaniel Swan, clerk, swore they were in his house in Alderminster from about 9 to 23 July. Then a tailor, John Welstead, produced his 'book', showing that between 9 and 16 July he had made a dust-gown for Mrs Hewit and carried it to her when she did 'pretend she was about going into the country'. Mrs Hewit and Mrs Holmes visited Welstead, in 1689(?), and 'pretended this entry was forged, and new' and then 'Mrs Hewit told him, if he did swear that, he would take off her brother's life, and Holmes's blood would be upon his head'.[27]

The two children, whose evidence, if reliable, proves the witnesses to Essex's suicide must have been lying, were William Edwards and Joan Loadman, both thirteen in 1683 and quite unknown to one another. They both claimed to have seen a razor flung out of the window of Essex's chamber which was then picked up. Edwards 'went to the Tower' on Friday 13 July instead of going to school. 'About nine o'clock [when] standing . . . between the lord Gerrard's, and the late lord of Essex's lodgings, [he] saw an hand cast out a bloody razor out of the said earl of Essex's lodgings; and [as he] was going to take up the said razor there came a maid running out of captain Hawley's house, where Essex lodged, and took up the said razor, which she carried into Hawley's house. [He believed] that it was the said maid whom he first heard cry out murder!' Joan Loadman when she was 'standing almost over against the late earl of Essex's lodging window, she saw a hand cast a razor out of my lord's window, and immediately upon that she heard shrieks; and that there was a soldier by my lord's door, which cried out to those within the house that some body should come and take up [the] razor; whereupon there came a maid with a white-hood out of the house, but who took up the razor, she cannot tell'.[28]

At the Privy Council and in Braddon's trial a great deal of time and effort was put into disproving the evidence of these two children. The argument was that both children were liars *and* that Braddon had made up William Edwards' evidence. William Edwards 'has used to come home with excuses for playing truant, to make lies on truanting'. Joan 'before that time [had been] taken in a lie'. Braddon's account, of how he had discovered the boy's evidence and why he believed it, was that on the morning of 16 July, visiting a Customs House officer, John Evans, he was told that the just published inquest report with its suicide verdict could not be accurate because of what a colleague, Mr Edwards, had told them his son had seen. Braddon called on Essex's brother, Sir Henry Capel, that evening and found him in 'great disorder under such a concern for so great a misfortune, as had herein befallen his family, that he hardly knew what he did or said'. So Braddon decided to act on his own. Next morning he called on Thomas Edwards. When the boy, William, came home from school and was questioned by Braddon, he 'denied all'. However when warned of the danger of lying he 'told me, that his sister's threats had frightened him into a denial'. Braddon came back to the Edwards' house the next day with written statements which the boy and his mother signed. On Thursday the 19th Braddon took the statements to the Earl of Sunderland, then Secretary of State, who 'seemed much surprised and told me, that I should bring [my witnesses] the next day'. When Braddon returned on the 20th he was taken 'into custody and some short time after I was called in before the then king and council', where he was cross-examined as to his motive and finally ordered 'to give bonds with two securities in £2000 a-piece'. Braddon was 'ordered to withdraw, the boy was then called in, and at first (as I was afterwards informed) did not deny the truth of his information; but being frighted by being before so great authority he wept; upon which his then majesty stroked him upon the head, and said, did not you invent this to excuse your truanting? To which the boy, trembling, answered, yes.' At Braddon's trial William admitted that he had signed the statement which Braddon had written and it accurately recounted what he had told Braddon. When asked why he had at first refused to sign, he answered because 'I was afraid for fear of coming into danger [because] that was not the truth'. He had *not* told Braddon this was the reason and had signed when Braddon 'said there was no harm in it', though his story was false. In 1689 William told the Lords' Committee that at Braddon's trial he had denied 'having seen the bloody razor thrown out of the window because major Hawley did threaten him, a little before he was examined in court, and told him, in great rage, that he ought to be whipped, once a fortnight for seven years' for making the report.[29]

Suggesting William Edwards had been lying was not enough for the government. They tried to prove that either Braddon or Thomas Edwards, William's father, had invented his son's story. A large part of Braddon's trial on 7 February 1684 was occupied in attempts to prove this. John Evans and Thomas Edwards were bullied and confused in cross-examination by the Lord Chief Justice, Jeffrys, who presided, by the Attorney-General, the Solicitor-General, and other judges. Even so Evans' evidence confirmed Braddon's account of how he had first heard of the Edwards' story. In spite of lengthy attempts to trip up Edwards and Evans they stuck to their story of the order in which Edwards had told Evans and Braddon of the boy's tale; and Edwards gave the same account of Braddon's approaches to the boy as Braddon did. 'Solicitor-General: How did Mr Braddon behave himself? Edwards: Like a civil gentleman. I saw nothing else by him, but that he was very zealous in the business, that is the truth of it, nothing could persuade him to desist.' Braddon examined both Mrs Edwards and her daughter during his trial to establish when and how William had denied the story which he first told. Mrs Edwards repeated the razor story and agreed that William only denied it 'two or three days after he had' first told it. There was argument as to what the sister had said to produce this denial. Braddon then called Anne Burt who described how Braddon had checked the details of his account by visiting the Tower. When asked why the boy denied his first story, she answered 'because his sister, as his mother told me, had been talking to him'. At this point Jeffrys stopped her reporting what the sister had said, because it was hearsay evidence! The prosecution's final resort at Braddon's trial was to produce another boy, Thomas son of Dr Hawkins of the Tower, who swore that he had been with William Edwards. He was examined by Jeffrys: 'Didst thou not see a razor thrown out of the window and a maid come and take it up? Hawkins: No, there was no such thing'. It then emerged, in cross-examination, that 'just before my Lord Essex cut his throat I went home'.[30]

The Privy Council had been busy in the previous summer investigating both William Edwards' and Joan Loadman's stories. Joan Loadman's evidence seems to have presented a greater problem for the government than William Edwards'. The Edwards family had made it abundantly clear to the Privy Council that 'none of them knew Joan Loadman'. Braddon told the Council on 5 September 1683 that 'three weeks after he had been with the boy he heard of a girl that said she had seen a bloody razor held out of the window and heard two groans'. The two descriptions were quite independent of one another and Joan at Braddon's trial stuck firmly to her story in the face of detailed examination by Jeffrys, the Solicitor-General, the Attorney-General and other lawyers. In the previous September the Privy Council had interviewed Joan, Margaret Smith her aunt, William Glasbrooke who 'was up two pair of stairs when [Joan] came in', and William Smith a barber whom Braddon had taken along as a witness. The three adults all agreed then and at Braddon's trial that Joan had told them the same story 'when she returned from the Tower'. Braddon had not offered the aunt or niece anything and 'ever encouraged the girl to speak the truth'. Glasbrooke told the Privy Council that 'he did not believe her, having found her heretofore in a lie'. At the trial he was more cautious: 'I have before taken her in a lie', but he could not remember that he had told Braddon this. Margaret Smith also told the Council that 'she did not nor does she believe the girl', but at the trial she did not repeat this. To refute Joan's evidence the prosecution picked on details in her evidence and called in the sentinels and Captain Hawley to refute them. Joan had said 'there was a coach stood just at the door', Russel 'there was no such thing' and Lloyd had never seen 'a coach in Captain Hawley's back-yard'. Joan had said that the razor 'fell within the pales; there is a door to go in'. Lloyd, asked, 'is there a door out of the pales into the yard', answered 'it is no yard, but there is a door that all pass through'. Captain Hawley claimed that 'the casement won't open above thus far; and it is so low, and the pales are nine or ten foot high, that it is impossible for any one to throw any thing out of the window three foot hardly'. Joan said 'a woman in a white hood came out, but I did not see her take [the razor] up'. Lloyd, asked 'did any maid go out of the house?, [answered] none at all. What, not in a white hood? No.'[31]

When we consider the awesome weight of political and legal talent brought to bear on the witnesses in the Privy Council and at Braddon's trial and the political atmosphere less than a year since the main Rye House trials and executions, it is really remarkable how little of Braddon's case was shaken. William's story may have been put in doubt but Joan Loadman's was hardly dented and Braddon's description of what he and others had done to obtain and check on the veracity of the stories had stood up to pressure. William's evidence at the 1684 trial was repudiated in 1689 before the Lords' Committee where both William and his sister, then eighteen and nineteen respectively, gave evidence. Either they were simply inveterate liars who turned with the tide or one of their accounts was true and the other lies, told through fear or to gain favour. If the latter explanation is accepted, it would seem most probable that the lies were told at Braddon's trial.

Braddon brought new witnesses and new evidence before the Lords' Committee in 1689. A Mrs Martha Boscomb deposed that 'a little before the death of the late earl [she] was walking before the earl's chamber-window, and hearing a very great trampling and bustle in my lord's chamber and looking to the window saw three or four heads move close together, and heard one cry out very loud, and very dolefully, Murder, murder, murder'. 'About a quarter of an hour after (or less)' she heard that Essex had cut his throat and was shown his chamber which was the one where she had seen the heads. Mr Perkins deposed that she had mentioned this a few days later. Braddon claimed: this 'is little less than ocular evidence of the murder; for my lord was a close prisoner, to whom (as was pretended, and sworn . . .) none was admitted that morning'.[32]

The third reason Braddon put forward for suspecting that Essex had been murdered was the extraordinary measures the government took to suppress the case made by Braddon and others and to destroy witnesses. Braddon's trial and imprisonment was the centrepiece, but there may have been even more sinister actions.

In 1689 the Lords received evidence of savage measures taken to silence people who suggested Essex had been murdered. A warder called Hawley, not the major, had foolishly told a friend 'that my lord's death was a piece of villainy' and at Braddon's trial hinted that he knew 'of that matter'. In the next month, March, Hawley was missing and six weeks later his body was 'found in a river near Rochester so barbarously treated and bruised, and his face altered that by his face none could know him. But his wife knew the body' from the unique way he wore stockings and 'a seer-cloth'.

While on bail in 1683 Braddon had renewed his enquiries, in particular asking after the soldiers who had been on duty in the Tower, the day Essex died. They were 'very shy, and denied to me, what they had before freely confessed to their intimate acquaintance, that the morning after my lord's death, their captain in the Tower commanded them, under severe threatenings, not to discover what they had observed'. Witnesses before the Lords' Committee in 1689 described how the indiscretions of two soldiers proved fatal. Two women deposed that on the day of Essex's death 'one Ruddle did declare that he was sure [Essex] was murdered, and that by the order of his royal highness [James, Duke of York]; for he did observe his majesty and royal highness part a little from those that attended them, and discoursed in French [which Ruddle having] lived many years in France . . . well understood. His highness declared, That of all the prisoners then there, the earl of Essex ought to be taken off; but his majesty said he was resolved to spare him for what his father had suffered; upon which his highness seemed very dissatisfied; and his highness parted a little way from his majesty, and then two men were sent into the earl's lodgings to murder him.' Braddon 'was informed, that this Ruddle was sent to the East Indies and at Fort St George, shot to death'.

A Mr and Mrs Bampton deposed 'that about one of the clock, the very day the late earl of Essex died, one Robert Meake (a soldier in the Tower) came to these informants' house, and [when asked] how the earl cut his own throat (with some earnestness and passion) answered, That the said earl did not cut his own throat, but was barbarously murdered by two men, sent by his royal highness'. Three different people swore that, a little while later, Meake had said 'that he did believe, he should be privately murdered, for what he knew and declared relating to my lord's death'. 'Meake was found dead in the Tower-ditch, and just over against major Webster's ale-house, which stood near Tower-ditch'![33]

Was Essex murdered?

Burnet who made public his belief that the Earl had committed suicide, nevertheless claimed that Essex was not guilty of the insurrection plan. Essex told him that he 'was glad that [Shaftesbury] was gone out of England; he had done them already a great deal of mischief and would have done more if he had staid. As soon as he was gone, the lords and all the chief men of the party saw their danger. So they resolved to go home, and be silent, to speak and meddle as little as might be in public business, and to let the present ill-temper the nation was fallen into wear out; for they did not doubt but that the court, especially as it was now managed by the duke, would soon bring the nation again into its wits by their ill-conduct and proceedings. All that was to be done was, to keep a good spirit with relation to elections of parliament.' If Essex was innocent of conspiracy but believed that he would not receive a fair trial it has been suggested that he may have taken his own life because if he had been condemned as a traitor his estates could have been forfeit to the Crown. However De Beer points out that 'the goods of a suicide were as much liable to forfeiture as those of a traitor or any other felon'.[34]

Modern historians have been influenced not only by Burnet but also by the fact that the House of Lords enquiry of 1689-90 apparently came to no conclusion although it was composed of four prominent Whigs, one of them Lord William Russell's father. Braddon explains that some of the four members of the committee were absent for most of the summer, 'But before lord Delamere had finished [his] intended Report, that parliament was prorogued, and the 6th of February then following [1690] dissolved. So that, in fact, there never was any regular Report made by those Lords of that secret committee.' The enquiry was not revived when the new parliament met. This 'argues that the Lords of that secret committee, did not believe, that all the proofs, by them taken, were sufficient to incline the House of Lords to believe, that Arthur earl of Essex was murdered by others'. Braddon suggests that this explanation of the Lords' inaction was seen as additional evidence that he had committed suicide. However Braddon did not believe it was the real reason; though he 'could not learn the true reason', he gave several equally plausible explanations for the abandonment of the enquiry. The two most cogent were:

'*First*, From all the Jacobite interest, as well protestant as papist'. Hardly any historian of the period would disagree with the assumption that almost all the leading political figures of the time kept some kind of contact with the exiled Jacobite Court as an insurance policy. To have found that Essex had been murdered would certainly have damned the Lords in Jacobite eyes.

'*Secondly*, King James the second, being father to the late queen Mary and queen Anne, it is natural to suppose, that neither of those two queens, would have had their father stigmatized, with that most infamous character of being a murderer . . . And whether king William, out of respect to his queen, might any ways hinder the fixing such an infamy upon his queen's father, I cannot tell. [But] queen Anne . . . struck me out of the civil list: Because as Her Majesty then said, I had thrown blood in her father's face.' Braddon made 'one reasonable request to all my readers . . . That they will ground their belief, of the manner of my lord of Essex's death, upon such evidence as to them shall appear rational'. His only reward was appointment in 1695 as solicitor to the wine licence office, which post was worth £100 pa. Two of his later published works suggest a social conscience. *The miseries of the poor are a national sin, shame and danger*, published in 1717, argued for guardians of the poor and inspectors to encourage arts and manufactures. In 1722 he published *Particular Answers to the most material objections made to the proposals for relieving the poor*.[35]

Was Braddon right? Or was Burnet and the historians who have followed him? Did the Earl of Essex commit suicide or was he murdered? There cannot be any absolutely certain answer. Not only is the evidence circumstantial, sometimes second hand, and based on rumour, but the state of public affairs in 1683 and 1689 was such that many people had a vested interest in avoiding unpleasant, even dangerous, truths, while others could see advantages in being forsworn. The reader in judging which way the balance of the evidence falls needs to remember the immense importance of Essex's death in the political situation of the 1680s. Two possible reasons for suicide have been put forward: that by taking his own life Essex saved his estate for his heirs, which was not true; or that he was in fact guilty and did not want to face a trial. The explanation that Essex knew he was guilty certainly suited the authorities, who immediately made use of Essex's death in Lord William Russell's trial. As Sir John Hawles, Solicitor-General in the reign of William III put it: 'they were sensible the evidence against my lord Russell was very defective, and that accident was to help it out; it was only slily insinuated [that Essex had] killed himself which had its effect, if the report be true of some of the jurymen's saying, "it went further with them than all the evidence of the witnesses produced".'[36]

Who might have murdered the Earl of Essex?

If the Earl of Essex *was* murdered, Major Webster, the alehouse keeper, and a certain John Holland *may* have been the assassins, each serving a different principal: Webster, the Duke of York, and Holland, the Earl of Sunderland. In 1689 Samuel Story deposed that the sentinel, Lloyd, had 'declared, That by special order of major Hawley, or one of my lord's warders, he did let in two or three men into the earl's lodgings just before his death; and he was very sure that major Webster was one': 'major Webster did confess, that he threw that razor out of my lord's window under such a consternation, that he knew not what he did'. Braddon argued further that there was evidence that Webster had produced 'my lord's bloody pocket handkerchief the very day my lord died, and that handkerchief was known by the E and coronet upon it; the very next day Webster produced a knit purse, out of which he told forty-nine guineas; it is proved that before that time Webster was very poor'. Mary Johnson, the 'labouring woman to Major Hawley', was dead in 1689, but her husband and another witness gave evidence before a JP that Mary had been ordered by Major Hawley to assist 'a man (to the best of his memory his name is major Webster) to strip the said earl from his cloaths'. Later 'she washed the said earl's body'.[37]

John Holland, according to Braddon, was one of the Earl of Sunderland's family servants, who heard Sunderland complaining that he could not trust any of his servants to do what he wanted. Holland volunteered and told 'an intimate' that this was Essex's murder and that he, Holland, 'was one of those who cut my lord of Essex's throat'. A certain John Waytis gave evidence that Holland often visited Sunderland after he had left Sunderland's service and was given money. 'Damn him, I have done that for his lordship, that he durst not do otherwise', Holland explained. This Holland became a common criminal; he was 'committed to Newgate' for robbery. The keeper at Newgate told the Lords' Committee that Sunderland's secretary, Montstephens, had visited Holland daily and paid him. Holland was found guilty but after his trial pardoned. He later committed murder and fled overseas.[38]

If Webster and Holland were assassins then the Dukes of York and Sunderland could well have been their principals. They may seem ill assorted bed fellows but Sunderland served James faithfully from 1683 until 1688. He has been described as 'the craftiest, most rapacious, and most unscrupulous of all the politicians of his age'. James' involvement in murder was sworn to, in 1689, by a more apparently reputable witness than Meake or Ruddle: 'a person of good estate, and reputation', Mr Peter Essington, described James sending two men to the earl's lodging who returned 'less than a quarter of an hour after, and as they came out they smiled, and said, The business is done; upon which, his highness seemed very well pleased'. In accusing James, Braddon was giving expression to popular opinion among Whig supporters as a report to the Privy Council suggests. 'Two traitorous rogues', Lumbard and Richard Allen of Richmond, Surrey were arrested in July 1683: 'Allen says that his Majesty and his Royal Highness were in the Tower about four or five in the morning the Earl of Essex cut his throat. Lumbard and Allen say the King and the Duke ordered a Jesuit to do it and that he did not cut his own throat, no more than they cut their own hands or the table before them. They say 'tis no plot but a trick to destroy the Protestants and cut off the principal men of the kingdom and of the Protestant religion and it is the King's and the Duke's design to bring in Popery as Henry VIII did the Protestant'. Braddon's investigations could hardly have been common knowledge this early, which suggests that rumour was already widespread.[39]

If Essex had not committed suicide, it was possible that Russell would not have been found guilty. If Essex had been murdered, the supposed 'Protestant Plot' was a nonsense, a 'Popish Plot' was nearer the reality. In any case the government of the day was clearly guilty of appalling judicial murders. Is it too much to suggest that plain murder was impossible? The late twentieth century historian has to shed the innocence which seems to have left earlier historians incapable of imagining that seventeenth century monarchs might be murderers. Can the difference in historians' reactions to the evidence for the Popish Plot and the Protestant Plot be because responsibility for the abuse of justice in the Popish Plot trials can be laid upon politicians like Shaftesbury and on popular hysteria, while Charles II and his brother, the Duke of York, cannot escape from at least some considerable responsibility for similar abuses in the Rye House plot trials?

Was the Duke of York more than the 'actual prosecutor', as Froude suggested, but also the instigator of a frame-up?[40] It would be naive of the modern historian to believe that seventeenth century Englishmen, who were willing to die and to kill for religion, were incapable of behaviour which twentieth century Germans and Russians practised for ideological reasons; in both centuries power may have been the real motive. The Rye House trials pale besides those at Leipzig and Moscow. The scale may be different but the behaviour of those in authority and of witnesses was not dissimilar. We have, after all, had the trial of the Guildford Four and the Birmingham Six in our own country and in our own day. Is it so impossible that James II, as he became, did in little what Goering and Stalin did in large, or that Judge Jeffrys could have acted like Vishinsky?

NOTES

1   Lawrence Braddon *Essex's Innocency and Honour Vindicated ...* (1690) p 4. In many quotations in this chapter passages have been omitted and punctuation modernised but without altering the sense.

2   The contemporary evidence is found in three volumes of Cobbett's complete collection of *State Trials:* Vol IX (1811); Vol X (1811); Vol XI (1811); abbreviated in these footnotes to *ST* IX, etc: the numbers following are of columns since these volumes have two columns a page and the columns, not the pages, are numbered; in the two volumes of *Calendars of State Papers Domestic* which cover the dates January 1 – June 30 1683 and July 1 – September 30 1683. These have been abbreviated in these footnotes to *CSPD* I & II, the numbers following are page numbers. These quotations come from *ST* IX 1132 & 1008-9

3   David Ogg *England in the Reign of Charles II*. OUP (1934 & 1955) 2nd edition, Vol 2, p 651

4   Lord Macaulay *The History of England*, edit by C H Firth. Macmillan 1913, Vol 1, pp 255-6; *ST* IX 396. Views of the plot appear in the following: J A Froude 'Cheneys and the House of Russell' in *Short Studies on Great Subjects*, selected by David Ogg. Fontana (1963) p 215; Ogg op cit *Charles II*, pp 647-8 & 651; Maurice Ashley *England in the Seventeenth Century*. Penguin (1952) pp 149-50, and *The Glorious Revolution of 1688*. Panther (1968) p 52; J P Kenyon *Stuart England*. Penguin (1978) p 221; and Lois G Schwoerer *Lady Rachel Russell*. John Hopkins (1988) Chapt. 5 & 6; Jonathan Scott *Algernon Sidney and the English Republic 1623-77*. CUP (1988) Chapt. 1 & en passim; and Richard

Ashcraft *Revolutionary Politics and Locke's Two Treatises of Government*. Princetown (1986) Chapt. 8

5   *ST* IX 375 & 403; G N Clark *The Later Stuarts 1660-1714*. OUP (1934) p 100

6   *CSPD* I 372 & 339; II 66 & 193

7   Ashley *op cit* pp 149-50; *ST* IX 1008, 385, 375-6, 392 & 399

8   Ogg *op cit* Vol 2, pp 647-8

9   *CSPD* II 26, 34 & 74

10 *CSPD* II 241-2

11 *ST* X 15, 9, 23 & 2; *ST* XI 356

12 *ST* IX 539 & 411; *CSPD* II 155; *ST* IX 553, 672 & 674

13 *ST* XI 879-81 & 883-5

14 *ST* IX 1241 & 1133

15 *The Diary of John Evelyn* edit E S de Beer. OUP (1955) Vol IV, p 326; quoted in a slightly different version, in *Hertfordshire Families* edit Duncan Warrand, *VCH* History of Hertfordshire Genealogical Volume, 1907, p 97

16 *ST* IX 124-6

17 Robert Ferguson, known as the 'Plotter', published in 1684 *An Enquiry into, and detection of the Barbarous Murder of the late Earl of Essex...*, which was reprinted in 1689. Colonel Henry Danvers published, in 1689, *Murther will out... the Earl of Essex did not feloniously murder himself, but was barbarously murdered by others*. In different ways these two could be said to be highly prejudiced. Ferguson was active in all the Rye House proceedings; he landed with Monmouth in 1685, was chaplain to the army and Monmouth's secretary, escaped and returned to England with William of Orange in 1688. Danvers had been an officer in the parliamentary army and became an elder of a Baptist congregation in Aldgate after the Restoration. He supported Monmouth but, as a republican, abandoned him when he claimed the Crown; Braddon's trial is reported in *ST* IX 1127-1224

18 *Essex's Innocency* op cit p 8; *ST* IX 1251; *Burnet's History of My Own Time* edit Osmund Airy. OUP (1900) Vol II, pp 398-9

19 *Burnet* op cit; *ST* IX 514 & 1282; *CSPD* II 202

20 *ST* IX 633

21 *ST* IX 1236; *Essex's Innocency* op cit, p 45

22 *ST* IX 1291

23 *ST* IX 1243, 1199 & 1277; *CSPD* II 136

24 *ST* IX 1243-5, 1199, 1201 & 1279

25 *ST* IX 1200-2 & 1269

26 *ST* IX 1285-6, 1283, 1289, 1282 & 1273-4

27 *Essex's Innocency* op cit, p 20; *ST* IX 1262-6

28 *ST* IX 1250 & 1253

29 *CSPD* II 337; *ST* IX 1186; *Essex's Innocency* op cit, pp 6-7; *ST* IX 1251-2, 1150-1 & 1322

30 *ST* IX 1143, 1173, 1180 & 1153-4

31 *CSPD* II 342 & 366; *ST* IX 1184 & 1186; *CSPD* II 371; *ST* IX 1181-2 & 1201-3

32 *ST* IX 1270-1

33 *ST* IX 1287-8, 1257, 1271, 1287, 1272 & 1287

34 *ST* IX 492; *Evelyn* op cit, p 327 footnote 3

35 *ST* IX 1328-30; *DNB* Vol VI, p 155; Mimeographic edition Vol 1, p 204

36 *ST* IX 800

37 *ST* IX 1269, 1280, 1281 & 1274

38 *ST* IX 1291-3

39 *The Concise Dictionary of National Biography to 1930.* OUP (1948) p 1227; *ST* IX 1273; *CSPD* II 234

40 J A Froude *Cheneys* op cit, p 215

PART THREE

RELIGION AND POLITICS IN HERTFORD
AND HERTFORDSHIRE 1699-1741

4

WHO KILLED THE QUAKER GIRL?
RELIGION AND POLITICS IN HERTFORD IN 1699

'Who killed the Quaker girl?' is said to have been the Tory election cry in Hertford well into the nineteenth century. The girl in question, Sarah Stout, died in 1699. Why should her death have had such a lasting influence on local politics? The answers lead into one of the stranger byways of party politics. Sarah Stout was the youngest and only surviving child of Henry Stout, a wealthy Quaker brewer, by his second wife. She was born in 1670 and had a half-brother, John, Henry's son by his first wife. On the morning of Tuesday 14 March 1699 the body of Sarah Stout was pulled out of the mill dam at Hertford. The coroner's inquest, which sat the day the body was discovered, found that the deceased drowned herself, being 'non compos mentis'. For the Quakers to admit that one of their number had committed suicide was a hard blow. In the murder trial which followed the defence argued: 'I beg leave to let your lordship a little into that matter, to shew you how this prosecution came to be managed with so much noise and violence as it hath been. I can make it appear, that one of the Quakers, Mr Mead by name, has very much, and indirectly too, concerned himself in this matter: it seems they fancy the reputation of their sect is concerned in it: for they think it a wonderful thing, nay, absolutely impossible . . . that one who was by her education entitled to the "light within her", should run headlong into the water, as if she had been possessed with the devil.'[1]

The agitation which followed the inquest on Sarah Stout led to four men appearing on trial for her murder at Hertford Assizes on 16 July 1699. They were Marson, Rogers, Stephens and Spencer Cowper. Cowper was the outstanding defendant. His father, Sir William, and elder brother, William, were the borough MPs. The family rented Hertford Castle. William, who acted as a kind of unofficial legal adviser to his brother during the trial, was to become Queen Anne's Lord Chancellor. Spencer became Chief Justice of Chester. Hertford townhall saw something quite out of the ordinary in July 1699, a future judge on trial for murder! This extraordinary trial took place because, as Spencer Cowper argued in his defence, prosecution 'was never stirred till two parties, differing on all other occasions, had laid their heads together'. The two parties were the Quakers with their religious motivation and the local Tories, the Cowpers' political opponents. The Hertford Tories were led by a medical family, the Dimsdales. Hertford had been a stronghold of Dissent since before the Civil War and the Cowpers' political control was exercised with the support of Dissenters. Henry Stout, Sarah's father who was dead by 1699, had been an important factor in this political alliance.

He was one of the first to join the local meeting of Friends in Hertford, after the visit of James Nayler in 1655: 'He was the first called Quaker who suffered imprisonment in the Hertford gaol, for the testimony of the truthe; where his sufferings were greate, the prison windows being shut that he might not have the benefit of air or of the light of day'.[2] One of the many pamphlet broadsheets which were published before and after the trial, one hostile to the Cowpers, gave 'some account . . . upon what occasion the acquaintance of Spencer Cowper and Sarah Stout began . . . The ground and rise thereof took its original from her father, who at all elections promoted the interest of the Cowpers, to the utmost of his power; through which a great intimacy was created between the families of the Cowpers and the Stouts; which did not expire with the death of her father; for her brother, by the father's side, continued his respects to that family, and spared no pains to espouse and carry on their interest, in order to their being chose parliament men for that town. . . when they were in the country, some or other of them were often together, as well the young women as the men.'[3] The Cowper camp's broadsheets tried to underplay this association, but some entries in the local Friends' Minute books of 1692 prove that there were, at least, business contacts. Before a list of 'Sufferings' at the end of one volume are some rather confused accounts. The first entry is a list of twelve items, headed 'Mony disbursted for Squire Cooper'. Below it is a reference 'to Squire Cooper's worke', and over the page is 'Received 2nd May 1692 of Henry Stout for the A/C of William Cooper'. The first two accounts total respectively £33.16s.1d and over £25. They cover what seem to be building works and farming. A separate entry is for £17 'received of him'.[4] There can be little doubt that there was a close association going back over several years between the Stouts and the Cowpers.

The political background

The significance of this association will be clearer when seen in the context of the bitterly fought politics of the Borough. Spencer Cowper, in his defence, argued that the real purpose of the prosecution was 'to destroy, or break at least, the interest [which means the political influence] of my family in this place'. The Quakers were encouraged by those who 'are possessed with much prejudice against me, upon feuds that have risen at the elections of my father and brother in this town'. The trial did indeed destroy the Cowper 'interest'. Sir William Cowper was first elected as borough MP in 1679 along with Sir Thomas Byde of Ware Park. From then on until 1690 there were changes in the local representation as a result of conflicts between the owners of local estates and the development of new 'party' loyalties. Who had the vote was a key issue, much disputed. The non-elected Corporation, named in a new borough charter of 1680, had the right to make non-resident freemen. What was in dispute was did such freemen have a right to vote for parliament or was the vote confined to 'the inhabitants, being householders, and not receiving alms'? A majority of the inhabitants were 'Whig' Cowper supporters. The majority of the Corporation were 'Tory'. A Whig broadsheet claimed that 'about the year 1681 . . . great numbers of clergymen, gentry and others' were made freemen so 'that the interest of the Corporation might be able to out-weigh that of the Borough', the inhabitants. These freemen had been allowed to vote in 1685 and 1689. The Whig triumph in the 1690 election made it possible for Cowper to stop the Corporation allowing unlimited numbers of 'outliers', as they were called, to vote.[5]

The Tory Corporation began its countermove in 1697 when John Dimsdale was made mayor. He revived the practice of creating non-resident freemen and 'contrary to the charter and usage of the town . . . continued four years . . . in the . . . Mayoralty the better to perfect the destruction' of the Whig vote.[6] In the 1698 election while John Stout voted for the two Cowpers, John Dimsdale's two sons voted for their opponents, the significant one of whom was Charles Caesar of Benington. To get away with a massive polling of outlier votes, Dimsdale had at least to weaken the Cowper hold on the inhabitant voters. When Sarah Stout's body was pulled out of the dam Dimsdale must have seen his opportunity. Rumours began to spread that she had been pregnant. Under the excuse that this should be checked, Sarah's body was privately exhumed on 28 April. Six doctors signed a report: 'We whose names are hereunder written, having examined the body of Mistress Sarah Stout, deceased, do find the uterus perfectly free and empty, and of the natural figure and magnitude, as usually in virgins. We found no water in the stomach, intestines, abdomen, lungs, or cavity of the thorax.'[7] At the original coroner's inquest John Dimsdale junior and a Mr Camlin, Sir William Cowper's surgeon, had given evidence. The signatories to the exhumation report included Mr Camlin, but the other five were all to give evidence hostile to Cowper at the trial. Three of them were Dimsdales, the mayor and his two sons; all three were doctors. The last sentence in the exhumation report was exploited by the local Tories. With other sworn statements it persuaded the Lord Chief Justice to commit Spencer Cowper and the other three men for trial.

The physical evidence at the trial

The trial, which contains much fascinating social history, centred around two kinds of evidence: medical arguments as to whether the condition of Sarah Stout's body proved she had died before or after entering the water; and attempts to show that the movements of the prisoners on trial, on the evening of Sarah Stout's death, were, to say the least, highly suspicious. Both sides called many 'expert' witnesses on the first point; there is a revealing difference between the prosecution's and Cowper's witnesses.

According to the indictment a rope had been put round Sarah's neck to choke and strangle her. Mr Jones, the prosecutor, in his opening statement: 'When her body came to be viewed, it was very much wondered at; for in the first place, it is contrary to nature, that any persons that drown themselves should float upon the water. . . Upon view of the body, it did appear there had been violence used . . . a crease round her neck, she was bruised about her ear.' Twelve witnesses to the finding of Sarah Stout's body in the water were called by the prosecution; expert witnesses followed. All these witnesses, examined as to the neck, agreed that the body had a 'settlement of blood behind her ear, as much as my hand will cover, and more; and she had a settlement of blood under her collar bone', but two were specific 'nothing round her neck; on the side of her neck there was a mark'. The younger John Dimsdale testified as to his examination of the body when first discovered, and his evidence followed the lines of those just quoted. There was a settling of blood on her neck, but no circle about it; 'No; not, upon my oath'. The prosecution's own witnesses had demolished the argument that Sarah Stout had been strangled.

The evidence about drowning was much less clear and was hotly contested. The aim of the prosecution was to show that Sarah's body had been found floating and that no great amount of water had left her body after she had been taken out of the water. The exhumation had found no water left in her body. The twelve prosecution witnesses disagreed among themselves a little but the picture they give is not really inconsistent. The body was found in the stakes by the mill-race, her head and right arm caught in the stakes. All the witnesses agreed that she floated; only three would be definite that any part of her body was above water; the others in varying ways described her clothes as floating and her body as 'about five or six inches' or 'three or four inches deep in the water'. Eight witnesses said they had not seen anything under her to prevent her sinking, but while one said the water was 'very clear', another said 'it was thick water'. Two witnesses said they saw no marks or bruises on her; none said they saw any. Four witnesses said they saw a little 'purging froth' come from her mouth and nose; they all agreed it was a little; one said 'I could hold it all in the palm of my hand'. Two witnesses agreed she was found tight-laced. Cowper, in his defence statement, claimed, scathingly, that his evidence was from 'the parish officers', not from 'obscure and poor men [who] have been taught to say generally that she floated . . they contradict themselves'. Only the clothes floated but the body was raised upwards by the force of the stream against the stakes, which sloped downstream. He argued that a body might be drowned by very little water, especially where voluntarily drowned. The two parish officers who had supervised the body's removal testified that only the clothes floated, as had nine of the twelve prosecution witnesses, and that she was firmly wedged in stakes which had, apparently, bruised her arm. One said there were sticks and flags under her and her legs might be resting on the bottom. They both said her nose frothed 'a great quantity'; 'as they wiped it away, it was on again'. One of the inquest jury was summoned and he stated 'there was no marks upon her, only a little mark about her ear, and something near her collar bone; . . . we desired Mr Dimsdale and Mr Camlin to see them, . . . Mr John Dimsdale told us, that these marks were no more than were usual in such cases, and it was only the stagnation of blood'. Two more witnesses testified to the 'great deal of froth'; one said it was the same as with a child who had been found drowned there earlier. Prosecution witnesses had compared this child's distended belly and body full of water with Sarah Stout's very different body.

It was the expert evidence, as to differences in the condition of the bodies of people who had drowned and of dead bodies thrown into the water, which produced the most lurid details and the bitterest arguments. Five doctors were called by the prosecution to give expert evidence on whether a drowning person will take in water and be certain to sink afterwards. Their evidence varied in its caution, but all went at least as far as Mr Babington: 'I am of opinion, that all bodies that go into the water alive, and are drowned, have water in them, and sink as soon as they are drowned, and do not rise so soon as this gentlewoman did'. Cowper by cross-examining elicited agreement that 'when the faculty of respiration ceases, no water comes in', but he could not get any expression of opinion as to whether there was any difference between drowning oneself and drowning by accident, though he pressed this point. The prosecution then produced evidence from two seamen as to the behaviour of dead bodies at sea. The clear impression was conveyed that such evidence, based on experience, was at least as valuable as the 'expert' scientific evidence of the medical witnesses. British sailors enjoyed a revived prestige because of the shattering defeat of James II's and Louis XIV's invasion fleet at La Hogue in 1692. It may well have been that battle which the sailor witnesses referred to in a gruesome description of battle and shipwreck. Their experience was that 'we hold it for a general rule, that all men swim if they be dead before they come into the water; and on the contrary, I have seen men when they have been drowned, that they have sunk as soon as the breath was out of their bodies'. As

Dramatis Personae

DEFENCE

Sir William COWPER, M.P.

WILLIAM, M.P. (later Earl)   SPENCER (later a Judge)
                             THE ACCUSED

MARSON, STEPHENS, ROGERS – other ACCUSED
MARSHALL – Sarah Stout's ex-lover
Dr. CAMLIN – Sir William Cowper's surgeon

PROSECUTION

HENRY STOUT = 1)   = 2) MARY STOUT
            (deceased)

JOHN STOUT

SARAH STOUT
(the dead person)

SARAH WALKER – Sarah Stout's maid

JOHN DIMSDALE
– doctor & Tory mayor

ROBERT – doctor   JOHN jun. – doctor

JONES – the prosecutor
MR, MRS & MISS GURREY – keepers of the lodging house
where Stephens, Rogers & Marson stayed on the night of
Sarah Stout's death.

PLACES – (see opposite)

BAREFOOTE'S COFFEE HOUSE (corner of Honey Lane &
Maidenhead Street).
GLOVE AND DOLPHIN (probably opposite Barefoote's).
BELL INN (corner of Bell Lane & Fore Street).
GURREY'S (near to Glove and Dolphin).
STOUT'S HOUSE (east of Christ's Hospital).
THE MILL DAM, probably not the Town Dam but Dicker Mill,
a 'corn mill', off plan to NE.

The Stouts' house was ¼ mile from the Glove and Dolphin
i.e. very near Christ's Hospital. From Stouts' house to the Mill
Dam and back to Glove and Dolphin took ½ hours' walking,
but even if it is Dicker Mill it is not much over 1 mile. Christ's
Hospital = 'The Buildings' on plan.

TIMES

AT STOUTS' HOUSE	AT BAREFOOTE'S	AT GLOVE & DOLPHIN	AT GURREY'S
Cowper until 10.45	A little after 11.00	11.00 - 11.15	c.11.00
MARSON, STEPHENS & ROGERS	8.00 -		

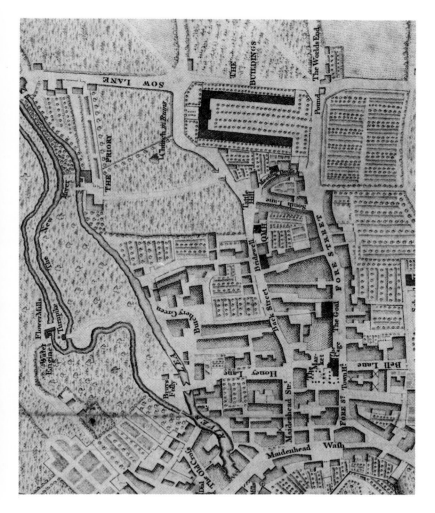

Plate 5 Hartford. Detail from 'A Plan of Hartford in 1766' by J Andrews and M Wren, from Andrew Dury and John Andrews *Topographical Map of Hartfordshire* [Hertfordshire County Record Office].

evidence that those thrown overboard float they argued that 'otherwise why should the government be at that vast charge to allow . . . iron to sink every man, but only that their swimming about should not be a discouragement to others?'!

A great deal of Cowper's defence was concentrated on trying to prove that Sarah Stout had drowned, that she had been alive when she went into the water. He called seven medical experts, London physicians professionally superior to the prosecution's mainly local surgeons, naval surgeons and Mr Camlin. Their evidence was that water in the stomach or bowels had nothing to do with drowning; it would only be present if a drowning person swallowed to avoid breathing in water. Drowning only resulted from water entering the respiratory system and a small quantity could affect this. Then they went on to argue that 'all dead bodies . . . fall to the bottom, unless they be prevented by some extraordinary tumour'. As to the sailors' arguments: 'The seamen are a superstitious people, they fancy that whistling at sea will occasion a tempest . . . I cannot think the commissioners of the navy guilty of so ill husbandry; but the design of tying weights to their bodies, is to prevent their floating at all, which otherwise would happen in some few days. Therefore what I say is this, that if these gentlemen had found a cord, or the print of it, about the neck of this unfortunate gentlewoman, or any wound that had occasioned her death, they might then have said something.' Two naval surgeons answered Sir Henry, Baron Hatsell, the presiding judge: 'When a dead body is thrown overboard, does it sink or swim? I always observed that it did sink. When we were in the channel, and in time of peace, we never threw any overboard but we put some weight to them; but it was not to make them sink, but for decency sake, that they might not be driven to shore when they began to float.' An indication of how seriously Cowper took the prosecution argument, which had been rehearsed in pre-trial broadsheets, is that the medical witnesses for the defence had drowned dogs to discover how little water was found in their lungs! These experiments were described in court.

Opportunity

Opportunity and motive were argued between the prosecution and the defence. As for opportunity the prosecution case was that 'Mr Cowper was the last man unfortunately in her company . . . it was a strange thing, here happens to be three gentlemen . . . I do not hear of any business they had here, unless it was to do this matter, to serve some interest or friend'. They had come to Hertford on 13 March, the last day Sarah Stout was seen alive. The detailed timing of events, as outlined by the prosecution, was as follows: 'Upon Monday the 13th of March, the first day of the last Assizes here, Mr Cowper

...came to this town, and lighted at Mr Barefoote's house, and staid there some time, I suppose to dry himself, the weather being dirty, but sent his horse to Mrs Stout's, the mother of this gentlewoman. Some time after he came thither himself, and dined there, and staid till four in the afternoon . . . when he went away, he told them he would come and lodge there that night, and sup. . . he came there, and had the supper he desired; after supper Mistress Stout, the young gentlewoman, and he sat together till near eleven o'clock. At eleven o'clock there were orders given to warm his bed, openly . . . in his hearing. The maid . . . went upstairs to warm his bed . . . she heard the door clap together . . . she came down, but there was neither Mr Cowper nor Mistress Stout; so that we suppose . . . they must go out together.' Sarah Stout was never seen again, alive. It was implied that Marson, Rogers and Stephens had met Cowper about 11.00 pm and helped him dispose of her and her body. However the case put by the prosecutor was slipshod if not self-defeating in its timing. Mr Jones argued that Stephens and Rogers had taken a bed for two at one Gurrey's lodgings; 'afterwards they went to the Glove and Dolphin, and then about 8 o'clock one Marson came to them there. . . they staid . . . at the Glove from 8 to 11. . . At 11 these three gentlemen came all into their lodging together to this Gurrey's. . . The people of the house . . . observed and heard these gentlemen talk of Mistress Sarah Stout.'

The first prosecution witness was Sarah's maid, Sarah Walker. 'On Friday before the last Assizes, Mr Cowper's wife sent a letter to Mistress Stout, that she might expect Mr Cowper at the assize time; ...as he came in with the judges, she [Sarah Stout] asked him if he would alight? He said no; by reason I came in later than usual, I will go into the town and show myself; but he would send his horse presently. . . She thought he had forgot, and sent me down to know, whether he would please to come? . . . he came in less than a quarter of an hour, and dined there, and he went away at four o'clock; and then my mistress asked him, if he would lie there? And he answered yes, and he came at night about 9. . . I got him his supper, and he eat it; after she called me in again, and they were talking together, and then she bid me make a fire in his chamber; . . . then she bid me warm the bed, which accordingly I went up to do as the clock struck eleven, and in about a quarter of an hour, I heard the door shut . . . and staid about a quarter of an hour longer, and came down, and he was gone and she.' In cross examination Cowper established that the Stout clock was half an hour ahead of the town clock. So the door shut at 10.45 pm. Cowper, in his defence, produced three witnesses that he had entered the Glove and Dolphin as the town clock struck eleven to pay a bill and stayed 'about a quarter of an hour'. It was a quarter of a mile from the Stouts to the Glove and Dolphin. Three witnesses, two of whom were knights, testified that it took half an hour's walking to get from the Stouts' house to the place where Sarah Stout was drowned and back to the Glove and Dolphin. Two witnesses testified that Cowper entered his overnight lodging, Barefoote's, 'a little after eleven'. There was no opportunity for Cowper to have done more than throttle Sarah Stout, even if they had left her house together. Since Marson and the other two had returned to Gurrey's lodging at eleven they could hardly have disposed of the body. The return at eleven had been accepted in the prosecution's opening statement and confirmed by the evidence of the prosecution's own witnesses, the three Gurreys, father, mother and daughter.

It would seem that the timing mattered less, at least to the prosecution, than it would in a modern trial. Perhaps this was understandable, given the inaccuracy of some of the clocks. Suspicion was cast on Marson, Stephens and Rogers because of their behaviour and conversation, as presented by the prosecutor, after their return to Gurrey's. There is a very significant difference between what took place according to Mr Jones and how his three Gurrey witnesses reported it. Mr Jones' version is as follows: 'One said to the other, Marson, she was an old sweetheart of yours: Ay, saith he, but she cast me off, but I reckon by this time a friend of mine has done her business'. Another piece of discourse was, 'I believe a friend of mine is even with her by this time. They had a bundle of linen with them', but what it was is not known [some of Sarah Stout's clothes were missing at first], and one takes the bundle and throws it upon the bed; "well", saith he, "her business is done, Mistress Sarah Stout's courting days are over", and they sent for wine. . . one pulled out a great deal of money. . . Saith the other, "thou hast had £40 or £50 for thy share": . . . next morning . . . Mr Cowper and they did meet together, and had several discourses, and that very day [they] went out of town; . . . My lord, we will call our witnesses, and prove all these facts.'

The Gurrey testimony was subtly different and much less damning. All three Gurreys gave versions of the conversation about Sarah Stout. Mr Gurrey: 'they asked me if one Mistress Sarah Stout did not live in town, and whether she was a fortune? I said Yes. Then they said they did not know how to come to the sight of her; and I said I would shew them her tomorrow.' Mr and Mrs Gurrey agreed the conversation had gone on, 'one of them said to Mr Marson, I think she was an old sweetheart of yours; Ay, said he, but she turned me off, but a friend of mine is even with her; . . . and *afterwards* [my italics] said, her business was done'. Still later he said 'Sarah Stout's courting days were over'. Mrs Gurrey: 'they had some discourse about money . . . somebody . . . say, the use money was paid tonight'. Miss Gurrey: 'Mr Marson asked the other gentleman how much money they had *spent*? [my italics] The other answered, what was that to him; you have had forty or fifty pounds to your share. Then the other asked him, whether the business was done? And he answered, he believed it was; but if it was not done, it would be done tonight. Then, my lord, he pulled a handful of money out of his pocket, and swore he would spend it all for joy the business was done.' She was asked and admitted she had heard no mention of Sarah Stout, in the part of the conversation about money. Marson, who defended himself and the other two accused, explained their conversation about Sarah Stout, which was not quite as the Gurreys had testified, as due to their friendship with a certain Marshall who had courted Sarah Stout eighteen months previously. Just before they left London they had been in conversation about Marshall and Sarah Stout. A witness stated that the company in London had in jest said, 'Pray enquire after Mr Marshall's mistress, how the match goes'. The money was fifty shillings, not pounds; it was Marson's fee for his work at the borough court in the morning before he left London. Mr Gurrey deposed that he had seen Marson and Stephens with Cowper the next morning; and two witnesses gave evidence that, after the discovery of Sarah Stout's body, Cowper had sent to the Stouts' house for his horse and left town without any further visit to them. Cowper explained 'it concerned me in prudence to send a common hostler ... for fear the lord of the manor should seize all that was there as forfeited'. This was all innuendo with no hard evidence of guilt.

Motive

There remained motive. Significantly the prosecution had not mentioned this but, as Cowper knew, broadsheets had. In his opening defence statement Cowper asked the rhetorical question, what motive could he, a man of good repute and careful living, have for murder. Sarah Stout was a wealthy heiress and the Cowper's enemies had suggested that Spencer had embezzled her securities, 'though not now, when I have this opportunity of vindicating myself publicly'. Cowper described one financial deal he had had in the previous December, 'the account of which I produced to my Lord Chief Justice'. He had, in fact, visited the Stouts on 13 March to pay over the mortgage money. In a pamphlet published after the trial it was alleged that Sarah Stout had loaned Spencer Cowper £1000 which he had misappropriated. The only reason, it was argued, that this had not been brought out in the trial was 'because their evidences that could speak materially to that point, were Quakers, whose affirmation will not be taken in criminal cases'.[8] Cowper's pamphleteer riposted: 'You say there are a thousand pounds wanting of her original fortune: I wish you had told us whether you set aside the charge of the prosecution . . . I suppose there was nothing spared to carry it on'.[9] Spencer Cowper continued his opening statement by arguing that his enemies by their improper exhumation had proved 'that there was no concealment of shame, to induce me to commit so barbarous an action'.

To make perfectly sure that he would be found not guilty of murder Spencer Cowper set out to prove that Sarah Stout had committed suicide. In doing this he dug an impassable ditch between the Quakers and his family. 'I shall give the clearest evidence that was ever given in any court, that she murdered herself'. To do this he produced seven witnesses who testified to her melancholy state over the past year; several had taxed her with it and three had been told it was due to love, where she could not marry. In one case, 'that cannot be, saith she: the world shall not say I change my religion for a husband'. One witness stated that 'she told me her melancholy had occasioned an intermitting fever'. Other witnesses testified she had acknowledged her melancholy when taxed with it and five witnesses that she had talked of suicide or the end of her life. These witnesses were shopkeepers with whom Sarah Stout traded, domestic and inn servants, and William Cowper's wife. There was an air of gossip about some of the evidence, but even watered down it cannot be washed away. Cowper then put Marshall, who had courted Sarah a year and a half previously, into the witness box. After receiving encouragement his proposal had been refused; was this on religious grounds? Two letters from Sarah Stout to Marshall were produced. Much earlier in the trial Cowper had in vain tried to get Sarah's maid to admit that her mistress had bought poison. He did get an admission that 'ever since last May was twelve months' she had 'had a great pain in her head' which made her melancholic.[10] However Jones then got a direct denial that she had ever been inclined to do herself a mischief.

The climax came when, with considerable cunning, Cowper exploded his bombshell, that Sarah Stout was in love with him and he was trying to prevent her acting foolishly. He opened with the mild statement: 'Now, my lord, if your lordship please, I proceed to shew you, that I went not so much voluntarily as pressed by her to come to this house, and for that I will produce one letter from her to myself'. The letter had been sent to a pseudonym at a false address, and Spencer Cowper brought evidence that it had been received by him and was intended for him. 'I am glad you have not quite forgot that there is such a person as I in being; but I am willing to shut my eyes, and not see anything that looks like unkindness in you, . . . I should very readily comply with your proposition of changing the season, if it were in my power to do it, but you know that lies altogether in your own breast: I am sure the winter has been too unpleasant for me . . . and I wish you were to endure the sharpness of it but for one hour, as I have done for many long nights and days; and then I believe it would move that rocky heart of yours, that can be so thoughtless of me as you are: . . . When you come to H-d pray let your steed guide you, and do not do as you did the last time.' This letter, dated Sunday 5 March, was followed by another, even more damning, dated 9 March. 'I writ to you by Sunday's post, . . . as a confirmation, I will assure you I know of no inconveniency that can attend your cohabiting with me, unless the grand jury should thereupon find a bill against us; but I won't fly for it, for come life, come death, I am resolved never to desert you.' William Cowper and three other witnesses, one a Quaker who did give evidence, confirmed that the letters were in Sarah Stout's hand-writing. In a strange departure from modern practice Sarah's mother and brother, who were in court, were shown the letters. Neither of them denied outright they were hers. Mrs Stout: 'How should I know! I know she was no such person, her hand may be counterfeited. . . I shan't say it to be her hand, unless I saw her write it.' John Stout: 'It is like my sister's hand. Baron Hatsell: Do you believe it to be her hand? No, I don't believe it; because it don't suit her character.' They have the sound of brave evasion; even though neither on oath nor having affirmed, as Quakers they could not tell an outright lie.

Immediately after reading these letters, Spencer Cowper put his brother in the witness box. 'I can bear my brother witness, that when he has been advised to make these letters, part of his defence he hath expressed great unwillingness, and has said, nothing but the life of these gentlemen could incline him to it.' The other three defendants provided a convenient excuse for what might have seemed ungentle-manly and unchivalric behaviour. William Cowper went on to give an example of Sarah Stout's unwanted pursuit of his brother, and to explain about Spencer's lodging on the fatal night. Barefoote's was regularly reserved for William during the Assizes but William did not know until the last minute whether he would be at the March Assizes. So the two brothers had agreed that, if William was not there, Spencer should use Barefoote's lodging. If William was there Spencer would accept Sarah's invitation. Spencer had told William: 'I would not willingly lie under too many obligations, nor engage too far; nor on the other hand, would I be at an unnecessary expence for a lodg-ing'. This extraordinary revelation of petty meanness in the circum-stances is the most striking of several hints that, while Spencer Cowper was innocent of murder, he was far from the spotless char-acter he tried to present. Too often he protested too much.

William's evidence was followed by Spencer's explanation of his movements on 13 March. Two witnesses confirmed that on arriving at Barefoote's in the morning he had asked whether his brother had given notice of his arrival; on hearing that he had not, Spencer had booked the lodging for himself for the night. As Sarah Walker had tes-tified, he then went to the Stouts' house, but only to pay over the mortgage money. He promised to come back in the evening, 'to go to excuse my not lying there'. He might have said he would come back that night, but not that he would stay the night, as Sarah Walker had stated. To explain Sarah Walker's evidence that he had not in her presence denied Sarah Stout's assertion that he was staying the night, and her orders to make up the bed, he requoted the last letter from Sarah Stout. 'I had rather leave it to be observed, than make the observation myself, what might be the dispute between us at the time the maid speaks of. I think it was not necessary she should be present at the debate; and therefore I might not interrupt her mistress in the orders she gave: but as soon as the maid was gone, I made use of these objections; . . . that my staying at her house... would in all probability provoke the censure of the town and country; ...but, my lord, my reasons not prevailing, I was forced to decide the controversy by going to my lodging.' This was really rather specious in view of Spencer's own clear admission that he would have stayed the night if Barefoote's had not been free.

The defence was over. Spencer Cowper produced the MP for Southwark to give evidence as to his character. Three witnesses testified to Marson's character, three to Rogers', and five to Stephens'; astonishingly one of Stephens' character witnesses was a juryman! When John Stout tried to produce witnesses to his sister's character, the judge refused: 'I believe nobody disputes that; she might be a virtuous woman, and her brains might be turned by her passion, or distemper'. After a brief and fairly well balanced summing up the jury went out for half an hour and came back to acquit all the prisoners.

The political consequences

The trial was over but not its effects. A flood of pamphlets followed and there was even an attempt to initiate another, private prosecution for murder. It was said that, in later life, Spencer Cowper was rather more tender than most judges of his time towards prisoners accused of murder. As late as 1728, when he died, he was remembered as Lothario in two poems. Sarah's fate was compared with Dido's in book four of the *Aeneid* and Cowper promised the same visitation in hell as Aeneas received.[11]

Even more lasting were the political consequences. Sir William Cowper stood for re-election in the general election on 3 January 1701, without his son; William Monson was his Whig partner. They were soundly defeated by Charles Caesar of Benington and Thomas Filmer of Amwell. Caesar got 445 votes, Filmer 344, to Cowper and Monson's 186 each. Sir William had anticipated his defeat. He wrote to his wife on 31 December 1700: 'I find a great change here for the worst, insomuch that I think our enimies need not pol(l)e honorary Freemen to carry their election'.[12] It was a long time before any Cowper contested the Borough again; it was 1759 before a Cowper was elected. John Stout, who had voted for both Cowpers in 1698, Robert, the elder Dimsdale brother, and Henry Chauncy, the County historian, all voted for Charles Caesar. Caesar was a splendid choice from the Tory standpoint. His father, Sir Charles, had been Knight of the Shire in 1679 and successfully re-elected in 1681 by the support of 'the gentlemen of the country [county]', in opposition to the local peerage.[13] As a 'Country Party' member he had actually had Quaker support in 1690. The son retained this support, strengthened by the events of the trial, for the rest of his political life, although he became an intransigent Tory and, after 1714, a leading Jacobite conspirator. Through some ten parliamentary elections, from 1701 to 1722, the Dimsdales and their ally, Joseph Calton, worked and intrigued for Tory control of Hertford Borough with Caesar as their front runner. John Stout voted for Caesar in three elections in 1701 and 1702; we do not know whether he continued his voting support after 1702. The Stouts and the Dimsdales were both new rich local tradesmen; the Stouts were brewers, the Dimsdales 'barber-surgeons'. The Stouts were on the decline; the Dimsdales were at the beginning of a remarkable rise to wealth and titles through their involvement with the advance in their profession. Collaterals of the mayor's family were Quakers. In 1722 John Dimsdale, the younger son involved in the trial, actually stood for election though he was defeated. In the years between 1701 and 1722 a continuous battle raged between the Corporation, whose mayors always returned Charles Caesar, and usually another Tory, as elected, and the Cowpers who did not give up the battle. They gave massive financial support to Whig candidates, though no member of the family actually presented himself as one. There were many disputed returns, always focussed on the issue of how many 'outliers', non-resident freemen, could vote. The Committee of Privileges of the House of Commons changed its rulings in the light of the political majority returned at each general election. In 1702 'all the freemen' were to have 'the right of electing'; in 1705 'such Freemen only as, at the time of their being made free, were inhabitants . . . the number of freemen, living out of the Borough, not exceeding three persons'. Interestingly, in 1715, the Cowpers were actually mobilising outliers to vote for their candidates, in spite of this 1705 ruling.[14] Charles Caesar's political career and the rise of the Dimsdale family are described in the next three chapters.

NOTES

1   *A complete collection of State Trials* Vol XIII, compiled by T B Howell, London (1812). All the quotations which are not otherwise identified come from the trial report on pp 1105 *et seq.*

2   Contemporary Friends Minute Book, quoted in C M Matthews *Haileybury since Roman Times* (1959) p 103. Henry Stout appears in later pages of Matthews, and in Violet Rowe *The First Hertford Quakers* (1970). Cp Joseph Besse *A Collection of the Sufferings of the People called Quakers 1650-89* Vol I, pp 241, 242, 248 & 250

3   'Some Observations', one of many pamphlets printed at the end of the trial report in *State Trials* op cit, p 1238, reprinted in *The Harleian Miscellany* II, (1809) p 250

4   Hertford Friends Minute Book for 1692. HCRO.Q.82 pp. 355 & 356

5   The disputes about the franchise and the electoral history of the borough are discussed in greater length in my 'Politics and Religion in Hertfordshire 1660-1740' in *East Anglian Studies* edited by myself, 1968, pp 117-145. I have drawn substantially on this essay for the present text.

6   'The humble Petition of divers Inhabitants...' HCRO, in Hertford Corporation Records, Vol 23, No 149.

7   Quoted in 'The Hertford Letter' and in 'Some Observations', both in *State Trials* op cit, pp 1216 & 1244

8   'Hertford Letter' *op cit*, p 1214

9   'A Reply to the Hertford Letter' in *State Trials* op cit, p 1235

10 Cp letter quoted in Matthews p 111

11 'Sarah the Quaker to Lothario', 1728. 'Lothario's answer', 1729

12 HCRO D/EP F23

13 Letter, dated 2 Feb 1680/1, from James Wittewronge to his father, Sir John Wittewronge of Rothamsted, Harpenden, Herts. HCRO D/ELW F29

14 Hertford Corporation Records, Vol 23 and *The Journals of the House of Commons*, Vol 13, p 709 and Vol 15, pp 54-5. See my 'Politics and Religion...' *op cit*

5

CHARLES CAESAR OF BENINGTON 1673-1741:
A POPULAR LOCAL JACOBITE CONSPIRATOR

The political beneficiary of the 1699 trial, the standard bearer of the Hertford Tory interest for which the Dimsdales worked so hard, was Charles Caesar of Benington. After 1714 he became an active Jacobite but retained a great deal of popular support in Hertfordshire. Caesar was a happily married man with a wide circle of friends. His life is fascinating for the light it casts on Jacobitism and on local electoral politics.[1] Charles Caesar was born in 1673 and died in 1741, bankrupted by the expense of his electioneering and his house building. He was the first eldest son in five generations not to be knighted and the first to marry into a County family rather than to the heiress of a City merchant. He inherited Benington Place in 1694; it had been the family home since 1614. Caesar's background made him an excellent choice for Hertford Tories to promote against the dominant Cowper-Dissenter Whig interest.

The family fortune had been made by Sir Julius Caesar who bought Benington; he was a judge who became Chancellor of the Exchequer and then Master of the Rolls. Sir Julius's father, Caesar Adelmare, half Provencal and half Italian and a Padua graduate, emigrated to England and became Mary I's doctor. Sir Julius's pocket prayer-book was handed down in the family. Charles signed a cynical couplet which he wrote inside the front and dated 1692:

'If Breath was made for every Man to Buy
The Poor Man could not live; Rich would not Dye'.

Charles made other, anti-Roman Catholic insertions. 'A Heavenly Wish' was a sarcastic quatrain in the spirit which was to dominate the eighteenth century.

'Reason doth Wonder, How Faith tells can?
Mary to be a Virgin! And God a Man!
Leave thy reason! Believe the Wonder!
Faith is above! And Reason must come Under.'

This was linked with a piece of heavy sarcasm on an indulgence granted by the Pope 'in the Jubilee of 1700'. 'Price Half a Crown. But not worth a Farthing. But only to Observe Fasting, misery, and Hypocriticall Cheats of Holy Rome. From Turk, Pope and Devil Good Lord Deliver us. Amen. Amen.'[2] These insertions are in marked contrast with the pious additions made by earlier Caesars. Charles' youthful anti-Popery might be remembered when considering his later Jacobitism.

Charles Caesar inherited more than a prayer-book and an estate. He inherited a political 'interest'. His grandfather, Sir Henry had, in

Chauncy's words, 'served this County faithfully in that Healing Parliament [the Convention of 1660] ... , was active there to suppress the Court of Wards and Liveries, and to ease the People of the Hardships and Charges which accrue to them' from the feudal rights of the Crown.[3] Sir Henry was re-elected to the 'Cavalier' Parliament at a by-election in 1666 with the support of local ex-Parliamentarians and in opposition to local Cavaliers led by Viscount Fanshawe of Ware Park. Sir Henry's son who was Charles' father, Sir Charles Caesar, was elected for the County in 1679 and re-elected in 1681 against the wishes of 'the Earls of Essex and Salisbury and Master of the Rolls'.[4] He was unseated in 1690 by the House of Commons: 'his return to be taken off the file, as his majority consisted of Quakers', who did not then have the vote.[5] The young Charles Caesar was,

Plate 6 Charles Caesar, 1673-1741. [British Museum].

therefore, an ideal choice as candidate in 1701 since he came from an established local family with a tradition of opposing the Court and the peerage; they were not Whigs but they already had Quaker support.

Charles Caesar the MP

We have seen how Charles Caesar won his first electoral victory, for Hertford Borough, in January 1701. He held the seat at the two following general elections, in November 1701 and July 1702, heading the poll. In 1702 he married Mary Freeman, sister of Ralph Freeman, the County member of whom Defoe wrote in 1704: 'Mr Freeman is master of all this part of the County [the north-east] as to parties'.[6] In May 1705 Caesar was re-elected, though support was falling; his fellow Tory Richard Goulston was unseated by the House of Commons Committee of Privileges in favour of Thomas Clarke, the Whig candidate supported by the Cowpers. In parliament Caesar took a High Tory stance. He was actually sent to the Tower, not his last visit, for attacking Godolphin, the leader of the government, during a debate on the Protestant Succession: 'standing up in his place, saying the words following: "There is a noble Lord, without whose advice the queen does nothing who, in the late reign, was known to keep a constant correspondence with the Court at St Germains"', the court of the exiled Stuarts.[7] Caesar's offence was compounded by his refusal to support the traditional 'County address because, he said, it applauded the administration', and instead pressing on Queen Anne one from the Borough of Hertford.[8] He was put out of the Commission of the Peace, ceased to be a JP, and defeated in the April 1708 general election.

The tide turned against the Whigs in 1710: Harley replaced Godolphin, in effect from 10 August. On 16 September Charles Caesar wrote to him: 'You having asked me yesterday what would be most agreeable to me, I let you know that nothing would be so acceptable as having Sir John Holland's staff or a Teller's place in the Exchequer, if either can be obtained for me; but I leave myself wholly to be disposed of as you think most proper'. Twelve days later Caesar wrote again with a note of urgency: 'Though I do not in the least doubt being put into some place, I can't help begging that what is intended may be done before my election, which will be on Wednesday October 4. Mr Goulston and I are both sure of being chosen by a great majority'.[9] Caesar's concern was because an MP given a government post had to stand for re-election. Caesar was elected in October 1710 but only appointed Under-Treasurer at the Navy after the election. So he had to face a by-election in 1711 which he won, as he did the general election in August 1713.[10] As a junior minister he would seem to have been popular with his subordinates. His wife, Mary, recorded in her diary an incident which happened to Caesar about 1736: 'the other day chancing into a common boat, the man looked earnest upon him (and though more than twenty years has passed) he said "Sir I am shure I was your servant when Treasurer of the Navy"; and whilst he was expressing his joy for seeing him, the crew of the Treasurer's barge came by in a shallop; and he was as soon huzza'd as the grateful waterman cried out "my boat is honoured with our old master, Treasurer Caesar".'[11]

Queen Anne died on 1 August 1714. The Hanoverian succession meant a return to power of the Whigs. In the general election of January 1715 the Mayor of Hertford, Joseph Calton, returned Caesar as elected, but he was unseated by the Committee of Privileges by a vote of 166 : 105. A Cowper was Teller for the Whigs, Freeman for Caesar. The Commons ordered that the mayor was to be 'taken into the custody of the Serjeant at Arms'.[12] The election had been bitterly contested. The Whig *Flying Post* reported that Caesar had maintained 600 persons at 'more than the common wages for labouring men for more than two months' and brought them to Hertford on 'the morning of the election'. 'Their usual cry was "No Presbyterians, High Church and Sacheverell, Low Church and the Devil"; and some of the gang were heard to cry in the night "No Presbyterians, No King George"'.[13] The Cowpers spent massively to defeat Caesar. The Panshanger papers contain an account of £1,122.13s and there are further accounts.[14] The mayor had given Caesar 373 votes, Goulston 362 and the two Whigs who were ultimately seated, 281 and 272. Jacobite demonstrations at Hertfordshire elections were not unusual. At the 1722 election for St Albans the agents of the successful candidates, William Clayton and William Gore, gave out the word 'Down with the Rumps! Down with the Roundheads! No King George's Justices!'. 'The mob was encouraged by Mr Gape junior who, with his drawn sword, began the riot on the election day, and caused the music to play "The king shall enjoy his own again"'.[15]

Caesar the Jacobite

Caesar was a close friend of Robert Harley, Earl of Oxford whose son, Edward, had come to live at Wimpole Park in Cambridgeshire some twenty-five miles from Benington. At some time after George I's accession, Oxford became, in effect, a Jacobite. Caesar joined the Harley circle to which Alexander Pope and Jonathan Swift belonged and was soon at the centre of Jacobite conspiracies. He proved a successful conspirator and was trusted on all sides. The judgement of some political historians is not born out by the Jacobite papers or by Charles' and his wife's correspondence. Keith Feiling described him as 'the very quarrelsome member for Hertfordshire . . . hardly fit to manage a wine club'.[16] Sir John Plumb, who should have known better, called him 'a rabid old Jacobite'.[17]

The fact is that until fairly recently historians have neglected and so misunderstood Jacobitism, leaving its history to the high priests of a romantic Toryism like Sir Charles Petrie. As the modern historian of Jacobitism puts it: 'History is generally written by the victors and little has been done to redress the balance of Whig rhetoric. Jacobites are always "rabid", Whigs are always "staunch".'[18] Caesar may have lacked political judgement in some of the advice he gave the Pretender, but he was liked, and not only by his watermen, and trusted by the Jacobite leaders, at least until 1729.

Historians now appreciate that Jacobitism in William III's reign and again in George I's reign was a serious political force. Caesar's accusation that Godolphin had been in correspondence with St Germains could have been made against many leading statesmen. An important group of Anglican clergy, the Non-Jurors, refused to accept William III as sovereign. In 1691 Sancroft who had been Archbishop of Canterbury negotiated with the exiled James II for the consecration of new Non-Juror bishops. Between 1690 and 1696 there were a whole series of Jacobite plots and invasion scares. In this atmosphere plotters new and old flourished. People who had been active Whig supporters became Jacobites. Robert Ferguson, 'the Plotter' at the centre of Whig conspiracies from 1679 to 1688, who was Monmouth's army chaplain in 1685 and sailed with William of Orange in 1688, 'changed to the losing side':

'Some truths are doubted; this by none is slighted,
There's no such fiend as Ferguson Jacobited'.

He lived until 1714 saying of himself 'he would never be out of a plot as long as he lived'.[19] Major John Wildman, one time Leveller spokesman, was dismissed from his post as William III's Postmaster-General, 1689-91, under suspicion of Jacobite intrigueing. William Bromfield, a Hitchin Quaker doctor, devoted himself to James II in 1687 and thereafter pursued a life of intrigue, plots and adventures in England, Ireland and France. R L Hine has told the extraordinary story.[20] Even more interesting is the evidence that the kind of anti-establishment popular activity, which carried on the 'Good Old Cause' into the 1680s, was after 1688 directed against William III and later the Hanoverians, becoming increasingly Jacobite in its expression. There is evidence of this in the Hertfordshire Sessions Records but more in other areas.

There was a hiatus in Jacobite activity during Queen Anne's reign but a furious revival on George I's accession in 1714. Lady Mary Cowper, wife of the Whig Lord Chancellor, commented in her diary on 'the riots at three several places on the Coronation day [20 October 1714] . . . These things did a great deal of harm among the common people'.[21] A modern historian, Nicholas Rogers, claims that 'during the opening years of the Hanoverian accession England resounded with riot and sedition'.[22] The evidence for the popularity of Jacobitism is widespread. One cannot help wondering whether the *Flying Post*'s accusation that Charles Caesar had 'maintained' the riotous crowd which supported him in the 1715 election was not Whig propaganda. The cost would have been considerable; they may well have been in the main sympathisers whom Caesar encouraged rather than the 'rent a mob' implied by the *Flying Post*. Charles Caesar's Jacobitism can be better understood when the popularity of Jacobitism in many different social circles is appreciated. His early adult life was a time of continuous Jacobite activity. Queen Anne's reign was to Jacobite sympathisers and High Tories like Caesar, a time of waiting. The Hanoverian succession faced them with the time for decision.

Caesar first appears as an active Jacobite in 1716 during negotiations with the Swedish ambassador, Count Gyllenborg, over the proposal that Charles XII should invade England to restore 'James III'. In January 1717 Gyllenborg and Caesar were arrested and sent to the Tower. The Jacobite papers make it clear that Caesar was 'the only person of all our friends who dealt immediately with Gyllenborg', but 'nothing material is found among Mr Caesar's papers'. He was released. Later in the year Caesar was the peacemaker between Lord Oxford and Atterbury, Bishop of Rochester. When Anne Oglethorpe forwarded Mrs Caesar's request for the Pretender's 'picture, an original in little', she added 'you know their merit and how useful they have been and are every day, being honest without any of the common alloy'. Oxford, supporting the request, wrote of the two Caesars as 'people of that consequence that ought to be encouraged to the greatest degree, for there are few in England so useful in the king's affairs; he spares neither money nor pains'. Mrs Caesar got the picture: 'She shows it to everybody and cannot be a moment without looking at it'.

A Jacobite invasion was in contemplation in the summer of 1717. Caesar writing to the Duke of Mar, the Pretender's Secretary, on 18/29*August revealed the strange mixture of commonsense and illusion which marked his loyalty to the exiled Stuarts. He wrote describing the unpreparedness and discontent of the army and navy: 'the Whigs . . . I believe . . . would now be passive, if not active, on a fair prospect of success. As to the Tories . . . you . . . may reasonably conclude their firmness will continue. Nothing but utter despair will, I

---

* The alternative (later) date given in the letters to and from the Pretender is the date according to the new, Gregorian calendar used in Europe from 1582. England adhered to the old, Julian calendar until 1752. So English dates were different (earlier) than European ones.

believe, ever alter them, . . . I cannot think anything could strengthen the king's interest both here and abroad, so much as marrying as soon as possible. . . . Far be it from any one to presume to dictate to his sovereign, but I humbly beg leave to say' that the king should marry a Protestant. But then, in December, Caesar wrote much less judiciously: 'if the giving up Port Mahon and Gibraltar would induce the Spaniard to send over six or eight thousand men from the Bay of Biscay with a sufficient quantity of arms, every man that has any duty for the king, or love for his country, must think those ports advantageously disposed of, were they of much greater benefit to our trade than they really are'. In the same letter Caesar added: 'in the present disposition of the people Roman Catholic troops would not give any manner of umbrage, the nation would entirely rely upon the assurances His Majesty has, and no doubt would give them upon that occasion for the security of their religion. In such a case the Irish would be the properest, if they could be got.'[23] Did Caesar really believe that no memories remained of James II's Irish troops and of the distrust created by James' shifting religious policies and promises? Had he forgotten his feelings as a young man when he wrote in the family prayer-book?

As with many other Jacobite plans the contemplated invasion never took place, but scheming continued and on 25 April/6 May 1720 Caesar wrote, sensibly, opposing the idea of a rising 'without foreign assistance'. However, when the South Sea bubble collapse at the end of 1720 improved Jacobite prospects, Caesar's enthusiasm got the better of him and he wrote on 28 February/ll March 1721: 'The affairs of the Court here are in very distracted condition . . . Indeed those who were the greatest enemies of the restoration think now nothing would be so much for their own interest.' By the beginning of 1722 Caesar accepted that it might be possible to restore the Pretender without the help of foreign troops. On 1/12 March the Pretender wrote to Caesar of his 'behaving himself in the manner which may conduce most to the success of this great undertaking'. This was the Atterbury plot, Caesar's part in which was to distribute military commissions.

Parliament was dissolved on 10 March and Caesar stood both for Hertford Borough, on 20 March, and for the County, on 3 April. He came bottom of the poll for the County as we will see in the next chapter, but he was returned in second place for the borough with 291 votes. Caesar took his seat and spoke against a bill which would have allowed the King to suspend Habeas Corpus. The mayor, Joseph Calton, had repeated his 1715 offence in returning Caesar and on 22 January 1723 Caesar was unseated on petition, in favour of Sir Thomas Clarke. Meanwhile the Atterbury plot was discovered. On 19/30 June Caesar wrote to the Pretender: 'It is from letters . . ., or at least copies of letters, that they pretend to have made the discovery of the plot as they call it'.[24] Atterbury was arrested, tried and in 1723 exiled by the House of Lords in an 83 : 43 vote. Caesar was in London at the beginning of May helping with Atterbury's defence and working with Lord Oxford.

After Atterbury's exile, and Oxford's death in 1724, a triumvirate managed Jacobite affairs in England: Charles Boyle, Earl of Orrery; Thomas Wentworth, Earl of Strafford; and Charles Caesar. Caesar continued writing to the Pretender until the end of 1729, though some suspicion arose that he had 'made his terms with the ministry' at the time of the 1727 general election.[25] On 9/20 February 1727 Caesar wrote of 'a war, which gives us here the only prospect we can at present have of your restoration'. He referred again to 'giving up Gibraltar' and described how a pincer invasion, in Lancashire and on the east coast, might be managed. On 29 June/10 July Caesar wrote another letter describing the effect on the Tories of setbacks abroad: 'the only way to prevent a considerable breach amongst the Tories... was to go one and all to Court, and as your steady friends are the most considerable amongst them..., it would... keep them undistinguished in the common herd'. This tactic might lull the government into false security and lead to the disbandment of 'a great part of the forces'. Caesar's attention to detail emerges in the comment of a Jacobite agent in London on 3/14 July that he had had 'not a sixpence, but from Lord Orrery and Mr Caesar... the latter is the only person that ever did handsomely that way'.

On 1/12 August 1727 Caesar wrote to the Pretender again: 'The duty I owe you, and the sincere concern I have for your safety, oblige me to beg of you in the most earnest manner, not to think of making any attempt here, at this juncture, without the assistance of a foreign force, which you seem not to have any hopes of at present'. This letter was written just as Caesar was making up his mind to stand in the coming general election. Parliament was not dismissed until 5 August and the County election for Hertfordshire was on 7 September. Between the end of July and the third week of August Caesar was sounding out what support he had. A meeting with the Harleys, Jonathan Swift and Alexander Pope on 29 July may have discussed his prospects and, maybe, even what Caesar should write to the Pretender. Caesar won the election, with Whig support, as we will see. Perhaps it was this support which gave rise to Jacobite suspicions. They may have been unwarranted as Caesar, in parliament, regularly voted against the government. However on 31 May/11 June 1729 the Pretender was informed that 'for several months past Lord Orrery, [and] Lord Strafford have observed that Mr Caesar has not been so frequently to visit, nor to communicate with them on your affairs as formerly,... there is strong presumption of Mr Caesar receiving money from [Walpole]. If there is anything wrong in Mr Caesar it is to be imputed to his great losses in the South Sea. His family is numerous and some of them grown up to be men and women, his creditors are very uneasy to him.' The Pretender was advised to continue writing to Caesar 'without communicating any secret'. The last mention of Caesar in the Jacobite correspondence is in a letter of 2/13 May 1731 written by the Pretender to Lord Orrery: 'Mr Caesar may also be coming soon into France... there were formerly some suspicions about him. I hope and believe they were groundless, but if you are not very much persuaded they are so,... be on your guard. However he is not to be shocked.'[26]

Charles Caesar's Finances

Robert Clutterbuck wrote that Caesar 'lavished away great sums of money [on his party], which brought on pecuniary embarrassment, and ultimately the ruin of his fortune'.[27] Lewis Turnor adds 'Mr Caesar was as unfortunate in his architectural, as in his political speculations. Having built an elegant modern house at Benington, on the site of the old family mansion, which he had pulled down, it was burnt to the ground just on the eve of its being inhabited.'[28] Caesar's fate was an extreme example of a process which, during the eighteenth century, weakened the squirearchy to the advantage of the peerage. The cost of 'keeping up with the Joneses,' rebuilding in styles made fashionable by the new large country houses, was more than the owner of a small country estate could easily manage. If at the same time he chose to stake a claim for local parliamentary representation his financial difficulties would be compounded. It hardly needed a disastrous fire to cripple Caesar. There were some who found a way out however. Caesar's Jacobite ally, Sir John Hynde-Cotton of Madingley Hall near Cambridge, was one. His mother was the daughter and coheiress of a Lord Mayor of London; his first wife, the daughter of Sir Ambrose Crowley, brought him £10,000; his second wife, Margaret, brought him one third of the huge fortune of her father and brother, the two James Craggs who had enriched themselves in government employment. Hynde-Cotton did not have a large estate, but he was able to spend considerable sums on major alterations to Madingley Hall, fight and win every election for Cambridge Borough from 1708 to 1734 and the County in 1722. The 1727 election was said to have cost him £8,000 and the borough thereafter complained of his stinginess. However the estate remained in the family and the eldest son, another Sir John, was married to the daughter of Humphrey Parsons, an immensely wealthy brewer, twice Lord Mayor of London and the brother-in-law of the older Hynde-Cotton's first wife.[29] The contrast with Charles Caesar is clear.

On coming of age in 1694, Caesar inherited an estate worth £3,500 pa. In 1702 he married into a neighbouring family; Mary Freeman brought him £5,000.[30] In 1718 Captain John Ogilvie described Caesar to the Duke of Mar as 'a man of consequence both for his good sense and his fortune of £4,000 a year'.[31] He lost heavily in the South Sea bubble (1720-1) out of which, incidentally, the two Craggs made a fortune. Caesar had taken £13,800 worth of stock *and* he had borrowed £41,824 against it.[32] There is no record of what he spent on politics but electioneering was not cheap. During the 1734 election, when Caesar was in debt, Frances Harcourt wrote to Mrs Caesar of some 'thirty people that will not go [to vote] unless they are certain of ten shillings a man for their journey'.[33] We know that the Cowpers who opposed Caesar in Hertford Borough elections spent large sums of money. Caesar fought the borough seat eleven times and the County four times, winning the borough nine times though being unseated twice, and winning the County twice. It was said that he had 'hoped to raise £5,000' for the Swedish conspiracy in 1717.[34]

Caesar looked for relief through the marriage of his son. As early as 21 March 1727 Lord Oxford wrote to Mary Caesar: 'I am told your son is going to be married to an only child and a great fortune. I hope it is true and that she has all other perfections'. The younger Charles Caesar's marriage did not take place until 1729. On 17 October Lord Strafford wrote to Caesar: 'I heard the news of your son's valuable match, but as it was only by the printed News, which of late are stuffed with lies, I darest not venture to send you my congratulations'. He did now, adding 'I dare swear [Mrs Caesar] had no small hand in the match though it was against the inclinations of her own brother; but such a brother! No one can blame her for taking care of her own son before his.'[35]

The 'valuable match' was Jane Long, daughter of Henry Long of Bayford who, Salmon implied in his 1728 *History,* was then dead while Jane was the 'present Lady of the Manor', though not more than fourteen.[36] Ralph Freeman, Mary Caesar's brother, seems to have been Jane's guardian and intended her for his own son, Ralph. However the Caesars organised an elopement which their friend, Alexander Pope, celebrated in the following humorous poem:

Upon the Royston bargain or Ale House Wedding
Marriage of Mr Charles Caesar to Miss Long - 1729

'Ye Fathers and Mothers
Ye Sisters and Brothers
That have a rich heiress in guard.
I'll tell you a tale
If you mind it won't fail
To preserve in all safety your Ward.

'Ne'er keep her at Hammells
In traces and trammels
Nor think an old man and his cat
   Are company fit
   For a girl that has wit
And is eager to know what is what.

'She's too frolick and gay,
To be tempted to stay
The return of a fiddling son;
   She won't feed on song,
   For her name is Miss Long,
And her business in short must be done.

'While Ralph and his spouse
Were employed in the house
With Wiseman their chief secretary
   Away went the gay thing
   In search of a play thing
And thus she began the vagary.

'Quoth he to his wife
"I'll venture my life
She's gone to the Ale house at Munden.
   And who can be there
   As I honour small beer
But Caesar aut nullus from London!"

'"I've told you dear Ralph
If you'd keep that girl safe
Ne'er trust her alone with Miss Cremer
   And as for Miss Jenning
   Her ways are so winning
She'll make her as gallant a schemer".

'Just as she said
Came in the poor maid
With message and face most importune
   That Caesar with forces
   And coach and six horses
Had stolen away their great fortune.

'"You see you old fool
You are made a mere tool
And duped by Caesar and your Sister
   You thought the girl safe
   By the care of son Ralph
But the booby crack'd walnuts and misst her".*

'Then out went the Scouts
  To the towns thereabouts
In hopes to have luckily found them
  But Saygrace, the parson,
  Had carry'd the farce on
And in Cottage had just before bound them.

'And then from her bed
  Having lost maidenhead
In the joyous and amorous strife,
  She cry'd "hang your master,
  I've felt no disaster
In passing from maiden to wife".

'And turn your face
  To Benington Place
And see with what joy this is taken;
  Where Madam does chatter
  To all that come at her
And cries "we have now saved our bacon".

'"Now my foes I despise
  Now my grotto shall rise
Though some folk may call it my folly
  And when all is sold
  The rest shall be told
Twixt Juleus, Betty and Molly".'

* 'This is a piece of True History "just come from Hammels". As the girls went into the garden the old lady would have her son follow them but he answered, "he would crack a walnut or two first".'[37]

It is quite probable that Mary Caesar's grotto building was an additional cause of Caesar's financial troubles. The correspondence received by both Charles and his wife contains many references to their 'Chapel, adjoining to the garden', 'the sacred Bower', and offers of shells for the 'Grotto'.[38] The runaway marriage did not solve Caesar's financial problems however. Freeman evidently tried to prevent his brother-in-law profiting from the marriage immediately, by insisting that Jane's fortune should not be touched until she came of age. Caesar took the matter to Court. On 23 October 1730 he wrote triumphantly to his wife: 'Lord Chancellor has put my son into possession of the whole Estate, has directed the Receiver and ordered him to pay my son all the money in his hands, which is all that the lands and money has produced since old Caryes death.† My Brother Freeman and nephew Elwes Counsel insisted that the receiver should

---

† Jane Long's mother was Jane Carey before she married Henry Long.

be continued in and that my son should be allowed but 400 pounds a year till his wife came of age; but my Lord say he could see no reason to take away 100 pounds a year from the husband to give it to a receiver; and they have had very severe reflections from every body in Court for the attempt.' No doubt the affair cost Caesar more money. There is a heartfelt cry in another note to his wife, 'God help those that are forced to attend affairs in Chancery. . . the aim is to keep my son out of his money as long as possible . . . I have overcome them all'.[39] His success did not put the family finances in order.

On 7 January 1732, Viscount Perceval noted in his diary: 'Heard little news, but the seizing Charles Caesar . . . his house and goods in town and country for debt . . . Mr Caesar was always looked on as a man of sense and fortune and had a very great employment under Queen Anne; his estate was £3,500 a year, and he was not noted for extravagance'. He lost the 1734 general election and, losing parliamentary privilege, was arrested for debt. He remained in a debtor's prison until 1736.[40] A letter written during the 1734 election is revealing: 'I am very much pleased to hear that my opponents chief dependance now is upon my not appearing in person at the Election nor having a sufficient Qualification, in both which points they will find themselves very much mistaken'.[41] Caesar was in fact defeated, but two years later, in 1736, Sir Thomas Sebright died and there was a by-election in which Caesar was elected. Lewis Turnor wrote of this as 'a remarkable instance of the esteem in which this gentleman was held by the county . . . the independent freeholders repaired in bodies to Hertford, and carried Mr Caesar's election at their own expense, by which means he regained his freedom'.[42]

Caesar was still an MP when he died on 2 April 1741. His will, made on 19 August 1740, 'is a melancholy memorial of the ruin of the elder branch of this once flourishing family. He desires to be buried at Benington, with as little expense as decency will admit', leaving to his wife, 'Mary, all arrears of rent which may be due at the time of his death, and such plate, jewels, and other personal property as may be free from debt'. His estates were left to three trustees; one was John Sabine of Tewin, another William Benn of Westmill, both political supporters. The trustees were 'to sell for the payment of his debts'. From the surplus £1,000 was left to Julius and £3,000 each to his two daughters. Mary, his widow, died on 12 July 1741.[43]

Charles Caesar's family circle

Charles and Mary Caesar were very human, with foibles and vanities which their correspondence reveals. They were happily married, devoted to one another and to their children, though misfortune was to be the children's lot. What stands out in the correspondence which the two Caesars received and kept is the affection shown them by so many people in the frequently catty circles in which they moved. They were the peacemakers. Robert Harley, the first Lord Oxford's feelings will serve as an example. He wrote to Caesar, on 6 January 1718 after his release from prison, thanking the Caesars for their kindness to him and for a friendship of many, many years. The sentiments are repeated in several letters: on 11 October 1718 Oxford wrote to Mrs Caesar: 'I had several advantages by being a prisoner, the chiefest was the many instances of yours and my excellent friend Mr Caesar's friendship'. On 12 December 1719 he wrote to Charles: 'my heart is thoroughly warmed with your friendship'.[44] When, in 1717, Oxford and Atterbury, Bishop of Rochester, the two leading Jacobites were at odds, it was Charles Caesar who acted as intermediary. On 20/31 May Anne Oglethorpe wrote to the Duke of Mar, the Pretender's Secretary, that Lord Oxford 'entering . . . into the necessity there was for the good of all the relations to keep peace among them . . ., sent a civil message by one Tavestocke [Caesar's code name] to Mr Flint [Rochester's code name]'. On 18/29 August Caesar wrote to Mar: 'The narrative you sent has dissipated the groundless jealousy Flint has got into his head that affairs were kept here as a secret from him'.[45] When Atterbury was exiled in 1723 he sent his farewell letter to Oxford through Caesar. The covering note read: 'I beg you to convey the enclosed . . . excuse me to Mrs Caesar for not sending her what I promised, but I hope to send it.

Adieu to you, Sir, and believe me ever

Your affectionate and most faithful humble Servant'.

This was written on 16 June from the Tower and endorsed as received on Friday 21 June.[46]

Lord Oxford was, it seems, godfather to one of the Caesars' children. On 22 August 1723 he sent Mary Caesar a present for his godson, adding 'I must desire leave to devolve the trust I took upon me into your hands'. Oxford was an ill man; he died on Thursday 21 May 1724. Charles Caesar was with him in London and wrote to Mary on the Wednesday: 'Poor Lord Oxford has been very ill since you was in Town and seems to be in a very declining condition. I have not yet told him what I came up about lest it should give him too much disturbance'. The next day, Thursday, Caesar wrote to Mary: 'Poor Lord Oxford died this morning about nine o'clock. You will guess by your own concern how much mine is for the loss of so great a man and good a friend.' Mary received two other letters which echo this estimation of Lord Oxford; they were both written on 1 June. Alexander Pope wrote from Twickenham 'I know you to be sincere in your concern for the loss of this great man, and therefore you will believe me so. . .The world is not worth living in, if all that are good in it, leave it for a better.' On the same day Francis Gastrell, Bishop of Chester wrote: 'the last great man in England is now gone and though his death is most lamented by his friends, yet in reality his country has the greatest loss'.[47] Gastrell had been Robert Harley's chaplain when Harley was Speaker in 1701. He and the Archbishop of York were the only bishops to oppose the Bill which exiled Atterbury. It may be he, then, became better acquainted with the Caesars, for Charles Caesar was in London with Lord Oxford assisting in Atterbury's defence. The reference to 'the last great man in England' is interesting. John Churchill, Duke of Marlborough had died on 16 June 1722, William, Earl Cowper on 10 October 1723. The leading opponents of the later years of Queen Anne's reign had drawn closer together by the 1720s. Was there a sense of having been the generation which had experienced great events facing replacement by their juniors, lesser men? Sarah Churchill, Marlborough's widow, wrote not unkindly to Caesar during the 1727 election campaign, as we will see. The Cowpers and Caesars had become friends as well as neighbours. Lord Cowper played a leading part in opposing the Bill against Atterbury.

In 1720 and 1721 the Caesars' wedding anniversary was celebrated in verse by their friends. Verses 'To Mr Caesar, upon the opening of his chapel, adjoining to the garden, on his wedding day' compared the Caesars' garden and its occupants to the Garden of Eden! Another poem with the same hyperbole contains the following lines:

'How great the peaceful comforts of an house
With a kind husband and a tender spouse!'

The family's history was summarised:

'On public good they ever fixed an eye,
And guarded both their King and liberty.
Eliza these adopted for her sons
Who were to be the guardians of her Crown.
By James and Charles they were as much approved,
As much were honoured, and as much beloved.
When Anna's danger taught her to beware
Designing Ministers, and to prefer
Her loyal Patriots, straight she thought on you,
Your merit, and your ancestors' she knew.
Without a pause she frankly did declare
That you should be her Navy's Treasurer.'

The anonymous poet ended with a hope for the family's future, for the next generation, which was to prove sadly awry:

'Then let the father in the sons survive,
And all the mother in the daughters live.'[48]

Charles and Mary had four children who lived to maturity: Charles born in 1704, Julius whose date of birth has not been found, Mary born in 1709, and Elizabeth born in 1714 or 1715. Mrs Caesar may have had miscarriages or other children who died in infancy, since there are several references in the correspondence to expected children, for example in 1718 and 1719. The eldest son, Charles, died on 14 November 1740, some six months before his father, literally losing his head in battle in Germany. Jane, his wife, had died on 11 April 1737. They left two daughters, the eldest of whom, Jane, married Sir Charles Cotterell Dormer of Rousham, Oxfordshire in whose family the Caesar papers remain. Neither of Charles and Mary's daughters married, perhaps because there was too little for an appropriate dowry. Mary and Elizabeth were buried in All Saints Church,

Plate 7 Margaret (Peg) Woffington, 1714? -60 *The Magazine of Art* 8(1885) p 257 [British Library, pp1931.pci].

Hertford, 'daughters and last surviving children of the late Charles Caesar, esq', as their tomb described them. Mary died on 19 February 1784, Elizabeth on 15 August 1790.[49] Julius the other son, of whom there is a charming painting at Rousham, rose to become a Major-General, 'never married, but bestowed his affections on the celebrated actress, Mrs [Peg] Woffington, with whom he lived in the most public and unreserved intimacy'. He died on 7 August 1762. Julius' career and life style seem to have followed those of Charles' younger brother, Henry, who had been 'placed in the military profession, and had the character of a young officer of much merit. He fell, however, a martyr to dissipation, and died unmarried in Portugal, of a consequent malady'. His will was revealing: 'I give to my well-beloved friend, Mrs Margaret Hopley, spinster, who now cohabits with me, my two cottages at Benington'.[50] Henry had died in 1706. Thomas, Charles Caesar's second brother, died in September 1727 just as Charles won his most sensational electoral victory. Dr Richard Mead, writing to congratulate Charles on 12 September 1727, added: 'I am very sorry that when I am to give you joy (as I do with the greatest satisfaction) upon the glorious success of your election, I should at the same time send you the melancholy news of your brother, the Colonel's death . . . Fever upon him which he had, as I was informed, contracted by taking cold upon physick – this threw him into violent looseness with a bloody flux which could never be stopped, and carried him off last night.'[51]

There were three occasions on which Charles Caesar was separated from his wife, Mary, for which moving letters survive. On 30 January 1717, when in the Tower, Charles wrote to his wife: 'I writ this morning to Mr Secretary Stanhope to desire that my dearest wife might have the pleasure of being a prisoner with me whilst I am one, but that is a thing not proper to be granted till after I have been examined . . . when that is over I do not doubt but they will be so humane as to let me have the comfort of a loving wife, if they do not set me immediately at liberty. . . I beg of my dearest to be as easy as is

Your loving husband.

My blessing to my children.'

Two days later, on 1 February, Charles wrote a second time to Mary: 'I have writ again to Mr Secretary Stanhope to desire my dearest may have leave to come to me, . . . the want of your company is much the worst part of my confinement. I have sent you a bill for some money lest you should want any for the family. I desire my blessing to my children and that you would give each of them a kiss for me.'

Caesar was separated from his wife again, in May 1723, when he was in London assisting with Atterbury's defence. He wrote to her on Wednesday 8 May: 'I think long to come to my dearest but can't till the beginning of next week. . . The Bishop's affair will not be over before Saturday at soonest.' On Saturday 11 May he wrote: 'I am very glad to hear that Julius is better and my dearest and the rest of the family are well. It will be a great pleasure to me to be with you next week. I thank you for the provisions you sent me; I intend to eat some of them at night with brother William and Mr Thomas. The Bishop's affair goes on very slowly.' On the following Thursday he wrote again: 'I will be with my dearest on Monday but cannot possibly sooner. . I have sent you two more protests and Kelly's speech in which you will find some very extraordinary things. The bill against the Bishop was passed yesterday in the House of Lords: 83 for it, 43 against it.' Caesar's correspondence with his wife was not purely domestic; he often wrote about public affairs as did her other correspondents. Mary Caesar was her husband's partner in political matters; her diary confirms the impression of the letters which she received; it contains many pungent comments on and analyses of her husband's electoral allies and opponents.

In September 1730 when Mary Caesar was at Bath, it would seem for her health, her husband wrote her two charming, purely domestic letters, which incidentally reveal Mary's keenness as a gardener. On 13 September 1730 he wrote: 'I fancy myself here like Adam before Eve was created, spending my time with the beasts in the field, the fowls of the air, and the fish in the waters, though he had this advantage over me, that not having experienced how happy a loving and beloved wife makes her husband, he could not be sensible of his want as I am who have for so many years been blest with one; but I trust in God you will come from the Bath hither in perfect [health] and then Benington will be a paradise for me'. A week later, on 20 September, Caesar wrote of 'Our Babes' being out; the babes must have been sixteen and upwards! The letter went on: 'I doubt not but they will think Benington, as well as I, a very melancholy place without my dearest, although the gardens and woods cannot possibly be in better order than they are. You remember the cock turkey when the fox had carried off the hen, clucked and tended those chickens he took no notice of before; so I, when I am not in the fields, walk about all day long with my spud and don't suffer a weed to peep his head up without immediately cutting it off . . . my sister is perfectly well ... brother William and all here at the Parsonage.'[52]

This was the human being whose involvement in the turmoil of eighteenth century electioneering we will look at in the next chapter.

NOTES

1   There is a long account of his role as a Jacobite agent in *The History of Parliament. The House of Commons 1715-54*, edited by

Romney Sedgwick. Vol I, (1970) pp 513-17, a biography to which I contributed. Charles Caesar is not in the *DNB,* though several of his ancestors are.

2 The prayer book, letter books, poll books and other Caesar documents, referred to in this and the next chapter, are in the possession of the Cottrell-Dormer family of Rousham House, Steeple Aston, Oxfordshire who are descendants of Charles Caesar. Charles Caesar's eldest grand-daughter, Jane, married Sir Charles Cottrell-Dormer. Mr Tom Cottrell-Dormer kindly gave me full access to these papers many years ago.

3 Sir Henry Chauncy *The Historical Antiquities of Hertfordshire.* 1826 reprint. Vol 2, p 81.

4 Letter, dated 2 February 1681, from James Wittewronge to his father, Sir John Wittewronge of Rothamsted. HCRO. D/ELW F29/4.

5 T H B Oldfield *Representative History of Great Britain.* Vol 4, (1816). p 25. The 1695 Affirmation Act allowed Quakers to affirm in civil cases. The application of affirmation to voting was not uniform. In 1697 seventy-two Hertfordshire Quakers signed an affirmation 'promise' of faithfulness to King William, detestation of the Papal power to depose Princes, rejection of any foreigner's ecclesiastical jurisdiction, belief in the Trinity and in the divine inspiration of the Old and New Testaments. This was 'subscribed... at an election of a Knight of the Shire... begun on Thursday 30th December' 1697. John Stout's was the first signature; very few of the seventy-two had to make marks. HCRO. Q PE 4.

6 *HMC 15th Report. Manuscripts of the Duke of Portland.* Appendix Part IV, 1897, p 154, quoted in *The Victoria History of the County of Hertford* Vol 2, (1908), p 40.

7 *The Journals of the House of Commons* Vol XV, p 70.

8 *H.M.C. Portland* op. cit. 13th Report. Appendix Part II, Vol 2, 1893, p 194.

9 *Portland* op. cit. 15th Report. Appendix Part IV, pp 595 & 602.

10 For fuller details of the elections in Queen Anne's reign see 'Politics and Religion in Hertfordshire 1660-1740' in *East Anglian Studies* edited by Lionel M Munby. (1968).

11 Mary Caesar's Diary, BL. Add. Ms. 62558.

12 *The Journals of the House of Commons* Vol XVIII, pp 136-7.

13 *The Flying Post* No 3601, quoted in W T Morgan 'Some Sidelights upon the General Election of 1715' in *Essays in Modern English History in honor of W C Abbott.* (1941, 1971) p 157.

14 HCRO D/EP F93.

15 *HMC. Report on the Mss. of the Earl of Verulam.* (1906), pp 118-19.

16 K G Feiling *The Second Tory Party.* (1938, 1951) p 19.

17 J H Plumb *Sir Robert Walpole: the King's Minister.* (1960) p 214.

18 Eveline Cruickshanks *Ideology and Conspiracy.* (1982) p 1.

19 James Ferguson *Robert Ferguson, the Plotter.* David Douglas, Edinburgh (1887); *DNB.* Vol XVIII, p 350.

20 Maurice Ashley *John Wildman: Plotter and Postmaster.* (1947) & *DNB* Vol LXI, p 232; 'William Bromfield 1650-1729' in Reginald L Hine *Hitchin Worthies.* (1932).

21 *Diary of Mary Countess Cowper.* John Murray (1864) p 19.

22 Nicholas Rogers 'Riot and Popular Jacobitism' in *Ideology and Conspiracy* op. cit. p 70.

23 *HMC. Calendar of the Stuart Papers* Vol VI, p 293; Vol III, p 538; Vol IV, p 301; Vol V, p 556; Vol IV, p 554; Vol IV, p 546; Vol V, pp 331-2.

24 Stuart Mss., quoted in *History of Parliament* op. cit. pp 514-5.

25 Dr William Stratford, canon of Christ Church, Oxford, writing to Edward Harley, 2nd Earl of Oxford, 20 November 1727, in *Portland* op. cit. Vol VII, (1901), p 452.

26 Stuart Mss. *op. cit.* pp 515-17.

27 Robert Clutterbuck *The History and Antiquities of the County of Hertford* Vol II. (1821). p 285.

28 Lewis Turnor *History of the Ancient Town and Borough of Hertford.* (1830) p 161.

29 *DNB.* entries for Sir John Hynde-Cotton XII. 305; James Craggs the elder XII. 439; James Craggs the younger XII. 440; and Humphrey Parsons XLIII. 402; *Madingley Hall, a Short History and Description.* Lionel M Munby. (1961; 1976)

30 'Notes on the Caesar Family', Ms. book at Rousham, compiled in 1881.

31 *Stuart Papers* op. cit. Vol VII, p 467.

32 *History of Parliament* op. cit. p 514.

33 Letter dated 28 April 1734 in Letterbook G in the Rousham collection.

34 *Stuart Papers* op. cit. Vol V, p 529.

35 Caesar Letterbooks E No 21; C No 8.

36 N Salmon *The History of Hertfordshire.* (1728), p 29; Clutterbuck *op. cit.* p 43 & 44.

37 Printed in *Additions to the Works of Pope* (1776) vol I, pp 135-8 and copied into an 1881 Ms. notebook at Rousham with the third and tenth verses omitted, a fascinating example of Victorian coyness.

38 Letterbook A Nos 14, 15 & 16 of 1720; Letterbook D Nos 40, 41, 42, 45 & 46 of 1723-4; and Letterbook E Nos 16 & 24 of 1726-7.

39 Letterbook F, under 23 October 1730 and letter dated Wednesday night.

40 *HMC. Mss. of the Earl of Egmont.* Vol I 1730-33 (1920), p 213. Turnor *op. cit.* p 160.

41 Letterbook C No 28

42 Turnor *op. cit.* p 160.

43 Clutterbuck *op. cit.* p 285; E Lodge *Life of Sir Julius Caesar... with memoirs of his family and descendants.* (1810), p 63. Lodge confuses Charles Caesar of Gransden with the MP.

44 Letterbook A No 5; D No 6; A No 11.

45 *Stuart papers* op. cit. Vol IV, pp 299 & 545.

46 Letterbook A Nos 30 & 31.

47 *Ibid.* D Nos 36, 50, 51, 52 & 53.

48 *Ib*id. A Nos 14, 15, 16 & 21.

49 Clutterbuck *op. cit.* p 164.

50 Lodge *op. cit.* pp 63 & 64.

51 Letterbook B no 38.

52 *Ibid.* D Nos 1 & 2, 33, 32 & 34; F, under 13 & 20 September 1730.

~6~
ELECTIONEERING IN HERTFORDSHIRE :
CHARLES CAESAR'S INVOLVEMENT IN THE
COUNTY ELECTIONS OF 1722-36

Eighteenth Century Electioneering

From the surviving Caesar correspondence of the 1720s and 1730s it is possible to get a remarkably detailed insight into how a county election was conducted in the early years of the Hanoverian dynasty. The availability of manuscript polls and printed poll books makes possible checks on how far people voted in the way they were expected to vote or had promised. Caesar fought four county elections in 1722, 1727, 1734 and 1736, a by-election. It is the 1727 election, his first victory, to which the most space is devoted in what follows. There were two 'knights of the shire' and every elector had two votes which made for complexities in voting and made possible complicated, and shifting, political alliances. With three candidates for the two seats each voter had six choices: he might use only one vote, a plumper it was called, for any candidate or he could vote for any two. In 1722 and 1727 Caesar, Freeman and Sebright were the candidates; so a vote might be C, F, or S, or FC, SC, or SF. This made possible the most intricate political bargaining.

Since no great landowner controlled the county, political power lay with the local gentry and the independent freeholders. In such a situation geography played an important part: each candidate tended to have his own geographical base [see Maps A & B].The east-west division was always an important factor in Hertfordshire history. So the same candidate might make different political alliances, bargains, in different parts of the county. It must be remembered that, since voting was in public and recorded and most electors, to some extent at least, socially and economically dependent on their better off neighbours, a promise to vote could usually be relied upon. Winning such promises, making an interest it was called, was the main aim of canvassers; and much contemporary opinion accepted that it was disreputable to break such a public promise once made or to attempt to persuade an elector to break it. We will see that these conventions were not always kept by some of the participants in these elections. However William Bucknall of Oxhey, who supported Caesar, wrote him two revealing letters. In the first, written on 19 August 1727, he said that while he himself was 'wholly disengaged, I wish I could say the same of the freeholders hereabouts. For not hearing of any opposition, I have not given myself any trouble to . . . make any Interest . . . I cannot say to one come and he cometh or to another go and he goeth, therefore I must see some of the leading men before I can be in any way sanguine.' On 23 August Bucknall wrote again: 'I have not been idle . . . I [did not] find near the number pre-engaged that I apprehended . . . [he] met with but few but have promised me for you and many of them single'.[1] These were the realities of eighteenth century electioneering, but there were some parallels with today's practices.

Caesar's Political Support

The two sitting 'knights of the shire' in 1722 were Ralph Freeman of Hamels in Braughing, Caesar's brother-in-law who had held his seat undefeated since 1697, and Sir Thomas Saunders Sebright of Beechwood in Flamstead, first elected in 1715; he held his seat until

Plate 8 Robert Harley 1st Earl of Oxford (1661-1724) [British Museum].

his death in 1736. Both, like Caesar, were High Tories; Sebright was a member of the Oxford Tory club, High Borlace. Freeman and Caesar had been close political allies in Queen Anne's reign. Their political paths separated in 1715. What persuaded Charles Caesar to challenge the county members? He had fought the borough seat at every election from 1701. On 20 March 1722 he was returned as one of the two members elected for the Borough but he had already been approached to stand for the County long before. His return for the Borough was contested as it had been in 1715; in fact he was unseated on 22 January 1723, as we have seen, and Sir Thomas Clarke, his old Whig rival, replaced him. A candidate could stand for two places

Plate 9 Edward Harley 2nd Earl of Oxford (1689-1741) [British Museum].

and choose which he accepted, if elected for both. A county seat was much more prestigious than a borough one, but Charles Caesar was nearly fifty and deep in Jacobite politics, not over rich, while county elections were costly. It does appear that the local Jacobites organised a coordinated electoral campaign in 1722. While Caesar stood for Hertfordshire, Edward Harley from Wimpole Hall and Sir John Hynde-Cotton of Madingley Hall, both Jacobite Tories, fought and won Cambridgeshire. Harley, an old friend of the Caesars, wrote to Mrs Caesar on 24 March: 'Had I not been at Cambridge, obeying your commands to stand for the County with Sir John Cotton, I should have answered your letter; you may depend upon my steward; he is for Caesar or nobody'. Two days later Nicholas Bonfoy wrote from Abbots Ripton in Huntingdonshire, heartily wishing Caesar success and promising to 'be with you on Saturday or Sunday at night, if it is only to Hurra for Caesar'. His letter continued: 'I have already got Lord Harley and Sir John Cotton some votes, and shall go tomorrow to Godmanchester Fair upon the same errand'.[2] Bonfoy may have been the Harleys' steward; he was married to the aunt of William Plumer of Blakesware, a Whig who became Caesar's main political agent in 1722 and 1727.

Caesar also had support from people who, while they may have been Jacobites, were fundamentally anti-establishment. Daniel Dodson of Cheshunt was such a man. He wrote from Waltham on 26 March 1722: 'I . . . have a just sense of your capacity and ability to serve your country at a time when it never more wanted the assistance of true Englishmen . . . I am sincerely devoted to your service and have already . . . summoned many of my neighbours. I am now going to mount my horse in further pursuit of your service and my own inclination which notwithstanding all names and parties shall never be separated from what I apprehend the true interest of my own dear country when in competition with a foreign one . . . [PS] let the odious names of Whig and Tory, high church and low church perish . . . now not them but England.' Such views were held in surprising quarters. Sarah, Duchess of Marlborough, spent money and effort in returning two Tory members for St Albans in 1722. She had become hostile to 'Sir Robert Walpole and the Hanoverian court'. On 2 September 1727 she wrote to Caesar, echoing Daniel Dodson's sentiments: 'I beg of you not to believe that 'tis anything of Party that is the occasion of it. For I have long since been weary of everything of that nature, having seen by woeful experience that the names of Whig and Tory have been made use of only to gratify the ambitious in both parties, without any regard to the true interest of the public'.[3]

What must have tipped the balance in favour of standing for the County in 1722 was support from an unexpected source, the Whigs. Sir John Plumb, commenting on the 1727 election, pointed out that

'Walpole always preferred an avowed Jacobite to a Hanoverian tory
. . . Governor Edward Harrison of Balls Park . . . whose daughter and
heiress had married Townshend's eldest son . . . a close friend of
Walpole . . . used his influence for Caesar, so did other supporters of
the ministry.'[4] Sir John's judgement was correct though some of his
factual details were wrong. Harrison's support for Caesar went
beyond Whig politics and the Whig alliance had begun earlier, in
1722, with an approach from William Plumer of Blakesware in a letter
dated 15 January, worded in a revealingly roundabout way: 'Sir, I have
ordered my servant to carry home one of your hounds who, having
been here some days and being, as he says, a good dog, I thought you
would be willing to have him. I was, a few days since, carried by a
hare very near your seat and had a great inclination to have paid my
respects to you; but as the approaching elections made people very
jealous of one another I did not know but my waiting on you might
have been some disservice to you, for which reason I declined it.
Otherwise I should have begged leave to assure you, as I now do, that
I shall always be ready and proud to do you any service I can be capable of, consistent with the obligations I owe to my particular friends.
When I say this I have no regard to my own particular interest; nor
any view but what I can fairly own, having determined not to attempt
being in the next parliament. I cannot tell whether you intend to be at
Hertford next Monday but, if I am rightly informed, our present members design to offer themselves again, one of them I suppose is our
representative for life. Sir, I beg pardon for thy trouble which, if what
I have said be improper, I desire may be taken as a letter about
hounds; . . . P.S. if now I am at home or any time hereafter you will
please to honour me with your commands, you may depend upon my
inclination to serve you in whatever I am able.'[5] The approach was
taken up and Plumer became Caesar's regular political correspon-
dent and election campaign organiser in 1722 and 1727, to oppose
him in 1734.

The 'representative for life' of Plumer's letter was Ralph Freeman,
the deeply entrenched Hanoverian Tory, the main obstacle to Whig
advance in the County. Once he was defeated the path might lie open
to a Whig victory and this is what Plumer achieved through a twelve
year campaign. Why Caesar did not see so far ahead is not clear.
Plumer was *so* active and effective on Caesar's behalf that the Jacobite
may be forgiven his delusion. That Plumer's 'particular friends' were
members and supporters of the Walpole-Townshend Whig government is clear. Edward Harrison of Balls Park had been the East India
Company's Governor of Fort St George in 1711. In 1722 he was Caesar's
fellow member for Hertford Borough but a Whig. In 1726 he became
Postmaster General in Walpole's government. At the by-election on 23
January 1727 George Harrison, Edward's brother, was elected. Caesar

refrained from opposition, as Mrs Caesar recorded in her diary: 'Mr Caesar thought it to no purpose to appear. Not that he doubted being returned but the alliance Mr Harrison had with Lord Townshend, Lord Lynn having his daughter in marriage, would have made his removal out of the House inevitable . . . Sir William Stanhope coming to Hertford spent a great deal of money, but gave it up, not being able to get Mr Caesar's interest; for he would not oppose the neighbour, though much solicited, and by Lord Essex who came and lay at Benington'. Essex had written, asking Caesar for support, on 24 October 1726. Caesar's refusal earned him Essex's opposition in the 1727 county election but won Harrison's support not only in that general election as in 1722, but also in 1736 when Harrison supported Caesar against his fellow Whig, Plumer's candidate.[6]

The 1722 Election

The 1722 county election campaign was in full swing by 27 March when Plumer wrote to Caesar: 'I wrote yesterday to Governor Harrison who sends me for answer that <u>he is very heartily at work for you</u>' [Plumer's underlining]. Harrison himself wrote on 31 March: 'We are labouring hard for you. [I] am ready to receive and execute any commands you will send me between this and Tuesday morning [polling day]'. Harrison had 'just come from London' where a meeting at the Crown had 'succeeded . . . beyond my expectation; I think we may depend upon two to the enemies' one from London, possibly three, and the greatest part single votes; some will go for you and Mr Freeman'. There were also some twenty to thirty unengaged freeholders 'at Coleshill in Amersham parish . . .; they expected to be sent to, and . . . would come on very reasonable terms'. This was a detached part of Hertfordshire in Buckinghamshire. Harrison asked Caesar how did he want voters to cast their second vote, if they wished to use it. Harrison's electioneering was not very successful as far as Coleshill was concerned: the only Coleshill voters who came to Hertford to poll voted: SF 4, S 2. However London gave Caesar a substantial majority, though not quite as overwhelming as Plumer and Harrison prophesied. Caesar had 120 votes, 88 of them plumpers and 24 FC votes, to Freeman's 106, and Sebright's 97; there were 82 SF votes, 8 SC and 7 S. [See Table 1]

In his letter of 27 March Plumer mentions one other notable local Whig who might support Caesar: 'Sir Robert Raymond, the Attorney General [who] lives at Kings Langley; he has an Interest thereabouts; I believe will not be against you, but I doubt [suspect] will be shy of appearing'. Raymond did not vote in 1722 and Caesar only got 5 of the votes cast in both the Langleys, Freeman 22, and Sebright 24. In 1725 Sir Robert Raymond became Lord Chief Justice. During the 1727 election campaign Plumer wrote to Caesar: 'the Chief Justice confirms the reports from those parts [the west of the county] of the inclination of the people if left to themselves. He keeps an exact neutrality'. In fact Caesar's vote in the two Langleys rose from 5 to 17 while Freeman's fell from 22 to 12. Another Whig influenced by Plumer was John Boteler of Watton Woodhall, MP for Hertford Borough 1715 to 1722, who had replaced Richard Goulston after a disputed election. As early as October 1714 he had written to Lord Cowper about the possibilities of exploiting divisions among the Tories to win the county seats. In 1722 he took action. Plumer asked Caesar whether he 'had wrote to Mr Boteler . . . he was very pressing with me to stand . . . he assured me he would come into any opposition'. In 1722 Boteler gave Caesar a plumper vote and Watton gave Caesar 26 votes, three of which were FC, but there were no other votes for Freeman and none for Sebright. Plumer mentioned another nine people who might support Caesar, five of whom he described as Tories, one of them 'at present not engaged'. Plumer was too optimistic: three of the nine did not vote and the other six all voted SF. When the poll took place on 3 April 1722 Caesar was not as successful as were Harley and Hynde-Cotton in Cambridgeshire, though he came close to Sebright. The voting was Freeman 1614, Sebright 1464 and Caesar 1340; in all 2762 people voted [Table 2]. Plumer wrote, consolingly, the next day: 'Nobody can be more concerned at the disappointment you have met with than I am . . . So good an interest made in so short a time, notwithstanding the violence of the opposition very well shews how great an esteem your county has for you'. Plumer went on to argue that the freeholder voters had been tricked and bullied against their real wishes. He added, significantly: 'I could be very well pleased to have a prospect of serving you more successfully but seven years is such a distance . . . but if anything should in the meantime fall out you shall upon all occasions find me . . .'.[7]

The Reversal of Fortune in 1727

Something extraordinary did fall out: George I died on 11 June 1727 and a general election followed with the Hertfordshire poll taken on 7 September. Caesar headed the poll with 2021 votes to Sebright's 1424 and Freeman's mere 1012. How did this extraordinary transformation occur? Caesar had the same wide political support as in 1722 and support from new people and new groups. The overall poll was higher in 1727 than in 1722: 367 more people voted.

Caesar's vote increased by 51%, Sebright almost held his support, but Freeman's vote fell by 37%. In both elections the solid core of Caesar's support was in his plumper votes: 948 out of 1340 in 1722 and 1515 out of 2021 in 1727. Sebright and Freeman relied on a joint vote: 1274 SF votes were cast in 1722, only 822 in 1727. A simple sum will show that, even in 1722, splitting this vote could have meant the defeat of either candidate, certainly of Sebright who was the most vulnerable. If 125 of these joint votes had become Freeman plumpers or if, as few as, 63 had become joint Freeman-Caesar votes, Caesar would have been elected. Caesar's tactics in 1727 were obvious. His enormous, and enormously increased, plumper vote by itself overtopped all Sebright's support. Plumper votes had the advantage that the second vote could, in theory, be swung behind another candidate and, so, used as a powerful bargaining counter. While Sebright was in the weakest position to face Caesar's challenge, it was Freeman, Caesar's brother-in-law, who was defeated, and soundly. The brothers-in-law certainly disagreed about politics and may have been personally at odds, but Freeman was clearly the target of the Whigs, as we will see. It was, primarily, to remove Freeman that the Whigs worked for Caesar.

A key intermediary between Caesar and Sebright was Robinson Lytton of Knebworth who had voted SF in 1722 but was to vote SC in 1727. The first mention, in the Caesar correspondence, of the approaching county election is in a letter from Lytton, dated 27 July: 'I don't perceive by your letter that you are as yet come to any resolution in relation to the county affair. I have sent to several parts hereabouts and find them with great cheerfulness ready to serve you. . . When you have determined, either to stand or not, be pleased to communicate it to' the undersigned. Lytton had a hand in arranging Sebright's defection. On 20 August Plumer advised Caesar: 'pray do not declare without Mr Lytton's approbation'; on 23 August Plumer hoped 'Mr Lytton will let you make your interest single as much as you can'. On 29 August he rejoiced: 'I hear . . . that single votes were making for Sir Thomas Sebright near his own parts; may it prove true'. On the same day John Byde of Stanstead, Plumer's cousin, wrote of Caesar's 'Interest in these parts improving daily; [if the west of the County was as good] I should, with much pleasure to myself, apply to Freeman, what Horace says speaking of an old raw horse, beat at last *Peccet ad extremum ridendus, et ilia ducit* [He fails at the end, mocked and broken winded]. Plumer's next letter, dated 31 August, reported 'that Sir Thomas Sebright was to be with Mr Lytton this week. I wish Mr Lytton could make him sensible how much it was his interest to take care of himself. If Sir Thomas pleases to put it in our power we can easily secure him.' On 2 September Plumer wrote to Mary Caesar: 'I am sorry to hear the news from Tring . . . I doubt [fear] if affairs alter about Tring Sir Thomas Sebright will not listen to our proposal; if not I hope Mr Lytton will consent his men shall poll single'. From the votes cast Lytton clearly did, but that Sebright was deaf to whatever proposals were put to him seems doubtful. In his own area he certainly switched votes [see Table 3A]: SF votes fell 235 : 87 and SC votes rose 6 : 103. There was a parallel vote switch in the

St Albans area [see Table 3B]: SF votes fell by 40 and SC votes rose by 52. Lytton at any rate appears to have trusted Sebright. He wrote to Caesar just before polling day, 7 September: 'I have not heard a word from Sir Thomas Sebright since I saw your lady [Mary Caesar], but believe all goes well, and shall have a true account of that matter as soon as I meet Mr Ashby at Hertford'.[8] Thomas Ashby voted S both in 1722 and 1727.

In Lytton's own territory [see Table 3C], Graveley, Stevenage and Knebworth, Freeman's 1722 vote of 59 fell to 7, Sebright's of 67 fell to 18, while Caesar's, of 41, rose to 95. Caesar's plumpers rose while the SF vote fell. What is odd is that the Lyttons had not supported Caesar strongly in 1722. Both Robinson Lytton and the Reverend William Lytton had voted SF. Yet Robinson Lytton had Jacobite sympathies, according to Edward Bulwer Lytton who wrote of the Robinson Lyttons as 'gay, spendthrift, idle roysters. Happily they lasted only two generations . . . In Parliamentary politics they meddled not over-much; . . . they did not condescend to acknowledge their Germanized masters on the throne; they were still true to the faith of the Cavalier.'[9]

'The Other Side of the County'

For pressure on Sebright to be effective, Caesar had to win more plumpers, and in those areas in which Sebright had the strongest support. This he did by active canvassing in the west of the County. The tactics of the election campaign, from the Jacobite side, may well have been discussed at a dinner party in Benington. On 28 July, the day after Robinson Lytton wrote his first letter to Caesar, Lord Oxford wrote from Wimpole: 'Sir, the Dean of St Patrick's [Jonathan Swift], Mr Pope, Mr Harley, and your humble servant design to dine with you tomorrow, being Saturday the 29 of this instant, if it be not inconvenient to you. – All our compliments wait upon Mrs Caesar'. For three weeks after these two letters, from Lytton and Lord Oxford, were written, the Caesar correspondence is silent. Caesar was personally canvassing for support and taking time to make up his mind whether to stand or at least to make a decision public. Five letters written to Caesar on 19 and 20 August make it clear that he had 'gone to the other side of the County'. On Thursday 17 August he had visited William Bucknall of Oxhey who was out; so he left a letter. On Friday 18 he wrote a first letter to the Duchess of Marlborough. On Saturday 19 Bucknall wrote back, wanting to help Caesar but unsure how much support he could collect. Plumer wrote the next day, Sunday 20: 'Your friends in these [eastern] parts begin to grow very impatient and want much to know what you determine . . . they have been told you was gone to the other side of the County and that a few days would determine whether you stood or not. I am asked every hour in the day if I have heard from you . . . I would only ask . . . whether I am to say you decline or . . . you have not received all the satisfaction which you expect from gentlemen on t' other side of the County.' On the same Sunday Richard Goulston of Wyddial wrote: 'if you are still feeling the pulse' there was strong support in Buntingford and Royston: 'sure I am, if you are so strong, as you hint, about St Albans, nothing can hinder you from being returned in Sir Thomas Sebright's place, for this side are lost people to his service'. Sarah Churchill wrote the same day that she could not 'give a positive answer'; while Edward Harrison wrote from London: 'I had some from St Albans' sides with me on Sunday', as though he had won their support. It must have been about this time that Caesar made up his mind to stand.[10]

Plumer was still pessimistic, writing on Tuesday 22 August of 'a great damp upon the spirits of our friends upon a relation Mr Freeman had just made of the ill success of your expedition to St Albans – in short that he was sure his interest stood stronger in those two Hundreds [Cashio and Dacorum] than it did last time'. In the event Freeman's vote fell by 186 in Dacorum and by 87 in Cashio, while Caesar's rose by 153 and 119 respectively [see Table 2]. Plumer went on: 'though I hoped it was not true, yet I own it made me uneasy . . . if the fact prove so, I cannot but think it impractical for you to carry your election . . . however I told the gentlemen you would stand . . . I have only to wish for a good account from the other side of the County to give me comfort and hope, as well as zeal.' By the next day, Wednesday 23, Plumer had heard from Caesar by letter 'which nobody here has seen but myself, nor shall I discover to anybody more of it than in general that there is a good prospect from those parts. I have heard nothing lately that has raised my spirits like it.' On this same Wednesday Bucknall wrote of his unexpected success in canvassing round Oxhey. On the Thursday Plumer wrote that 'the account from William Bucknall was a great cordial for me'. He went on to comment that 'the inclination of the men in the Dacorum Hundred' was surprising; if they persevered nothing could lose the election. 'I hope you will continue . . . to cultivate that good disposition . . . without giving offence to Mr Gore; if he proves neuter I think you are safe'.[11] While Caesar seems to have given most of his attention to the west of Hertfordshire, Sebright's territory, his friends and allies canvassed in the centre and east.

Geography was of fundamental importance in the electoral campaign because each of the candidates had distinct areas of the County, near their homes, in which their political control was overwhelming. This is what lay behind the references to 'the other side' and 'this side' of the County [see Maps and Tables 3A-E]. Sebright's control was absolute in fourteen places in the north-west, near his home, Beechwood in Flamstead. This was an area north of a line including Redbourn and the Langleys, but excluding Bovingdon, Northchurch, Puttenham and Wigginton; no votes were recorded for Markyate and Nettleden. Caddington and Kensworth, then in Hertfordshire, came into the area. Hexton and Lilley were Sebright supporters [Table 3A]. From Hamels in Braughing Freeman controlled twenty-one places in the east and north-east [see Table 3D]. What Defoe had claimed in 1704 that Freeman was 'master of all this part of the County as to parties', was still true in 1722 and 1727.[12] The area stretched north-south, from Barley and Barkway to the Pelhams along the eastern boundary of the County, and from Bygrave to Westmill and Braughing along a north-south line a little further west. East to west the area reached from the Pelhams to Baldock. No votes were recorded for Nuthampstead and Throcking. Freeman had most votes in 1722 in several other parishes in this area, but lost out to Caesar in 1727. Caesar's control over the centre of the County was the most remarkable; it extended over thirty-five almost contiguous places stretching from Cheshunt in the south to Offley and Hitchin in the north, omitting Broxbourne, Hoddesdon and Wormley; and from the Waldens in the west to the Hadhams and Gilston in the east, bypassing Standon [Table 3E]. No votes were recorded in Langley and Shephall. Robinson Lytton controlled the three parishes of Graveley, Knebworth and Stevenage in the middle of this area. In each region the home candidate had a clear majority of votes both in 1722 and 1727, *and* increased his voting support, though Caesar gained votes in both Freeman's and Sebright's areas. Most of the rest of the County can be divided into two different areas, politically; in nineteen places adjacent to either Freeman's or Sebright's home territories [Map B] Caesar, in the minority in 1722, won a majority in 1727. In these areas Caesar's vote rose from 224 to 405, Freeman's fell from 371 to 238 and Sebright's from 308 to 233. In ten places in the south-west of the County [see Map B], all three candidates' votes rose, but Sebright's much more than the others and Caesar remained in a minority. The voting was Sebright 92 : 142, Freeman 118 : 124 and Caesar only 61 : 70. Detailed analysis of the poll books reveals the county wide support which Caesar had in 1727 from very different types of voters.

The Quaker, London, and Urban Vote

Since the 1690s Caesars had had the support of Hertfordshire Quakers. Sir John Plumb was quite wrong in attributing this support to Walpole's bidding.[13] The Quaker vote is identifiable because Quakers affirmed when voting and the poll books were so marked. In 1722 their votes were Caesar 58, Freeman 51, Sebright 8. In 1727 there was a considerable switch from Freeman to Caesar: the C vote rose from 16 to 53 and the FC vote fell from 41 to 27. Caesar had 81 votes,

Freeman 37, and Sebright 5 [Table 4]. There was one serious attempt during the 1727 election to turn the Quakers against Caesar; presumably it came from Freeman's supporters. Plumer wrote on 22 August that at Ware market 'I met . . . a silly story calculated to prejudice you . . . in effect that some time since, you . . . discharged [a man] from your work, under one Rayment . . ., because he was a Quaker . . . [saying] you hoped they and Dissenters of all sorts would everywhere be rooted out.' Caesar must have sent the denial Plumer asked for the same day, for Plumer wrote on 23 August: 'I am sorry I was not in . . . when your tenant came, not that I wanted any satisfaction myself for I never believed any word of the story . . . I believe it was calculated for a bad purpose'.[14] Pressure to break the long link between Hertfordshire Quakers and Caesar re-emerged in the 1734 general election. Mr Robert Berry wrote from Hitchin on 24 April 1734 to his 'dear friend and loving brother', William Wilshere of the Frith, Welwyn, begging him not to engage 'to vote for Mr Caesar': surely Wilshere 'knew the interest of your country and particularly of Protestant Dissenters better than to vote for such a man as he, who I doubt [suspect] is an enemy to both'. Berry continued, at length, to outline the Whig version of how Dissenters had won 'civil and religious liberties' which Caesar, as an MP in Queen Anne's reign, had threatened. 'I earnestly and heartily beseech you . . . that you would have no hand in bringing such a man as he is into the House of Commons. If you should object to this and say why did the Dissenters vote for Mr Caesar last election, I answer it was to throw Mr Freeman out, who they thought having more influence in the House of Commons might do them more harm there than he; and not for any love they had to Mr Caesar.'[15] This has all the marks of Plumer's 1734 campaign and reveals the real motives of the Walpole Whigs who worked for Caesar in 1722 and 1727. It does NOT explain the Quaker vote, though it may be that other Dissenters voted for Caesar in the 1720s through Whig persuasion.

Another area in which Caesar's clear majority in 1722 was very much increased in 1727 was in the London votes, and here Whig influence seems to have been dominant. Caesar's vote rose from 120 to 153; the rise in the C vote from 88 to 125 accounted for all and more of this increase [Table 1]. Freeman's vote fell from 106 to 51 and Sebright's from 97 to 70; the SF vote fell from 82 to 43 and the SC vote rose from 8 to 21. The London vote needed careful organising. On 22 August Plumer asked Caesar to write 'to Alderman Parsons at London who I hear is your friend'. Humphrey Parsons, a wealthy brewer and twice Lord Mayor of London, was closely related to the Hynde-Cottons of Madingley. The *Dictionary of National Biography* describes him as 'an incorruptible tory'.[16] However the three most important people in organising the London vote in 1727 were Whigs: William

Plumer and his agent, Plumer's friend, Mr Roper; Edward Harrison; and the Radcliffes of Hitchin Priory who were leading Levant merchants. On 27 August Plumer wrote: 'Roper sends me word that he has done what he could in Town . . . The Governor came down last night; though he must not act himself, he is a proper person to consult about the method of managing London . . . I think to step to London tomorrow morning . . . if you have a list of Londoners to spare I will carry it with me, though I would not have you neglect other means of managing the interest there. Mr Radcliffe can probably advise how to manage at London, they having done it for their grandfather.' This was Sir Ralph Radcliffe who fought the County as a Whig in 1715, gaining only 1158 votes to Freeman's 1787 and Sebright's 1807. He had died in 1720. Edward Radcliffe had already written to Caesar on about 24/25 August: 'I suppose you are informed the Old Members had a meeting of their friends last night at the King's Arms in St Paul's churchyard'. Plumer wrote from London on 29 August: 'My agent in London has done some service and so has Mr Roper; but there is so much alteration by death or change of habitation, that I find it a vain thing to hope to find the people in this place without a meeting. Which whenever there is I have ordered my agent to attend and to be ready to answer any scruples and to do whatever services he can as occasion may offer. I cannot learn much of the meeting at Truby's [presumably of the Old Members' supporters]; only that about 70 were there and some disconcert amongst them.' On 31 August Plumer reported: 'I see a meeting of your friends is appointed for tomorrow night in Town'.[17]

Hertford and Ware had long been Caesar strongholds [Table 5]. They gave him 153 votes in 1722, 11.4% of his total vote, and 191 in 1727, almost 20% of his total urban vote. Plumer's support in Ware and that of the Harrisons in Hertford, plumper votes in 1722 and 1727, was important. They were not alone, however: Caesar had the voting support of other gentry. Even Sir Thomas Clarke, the borough MP and Caesar's long-term political rival, gave him a plumper vote in 1727. This was an important factor in the swing of support to Caesar in other urban areas in the County. In the eighteen most populous places in the County [Table 5], the 1722 vote was Freeman 746, Sebright 665, and Caesar 636; in 1727 Caesar 966, Sebright 595, and Freeman only 452. Caesar's biggest gains, always mainly at Freeman's expense, were in St Albans, Hitchin and Watford.

Caesar's Opponents: the Clergy and the Peers

It was in the many villages of Hertfordshire that the ultimate struggle took place and here what was decisive was the support of local landowners and resident clergy and gentry. The clergy and the peerage opposed Caesar; they were the only identifiable social groupings which did so. However the local gentry swung round in his favour and this was conclusive as we will see. While the clergy clearly could make a local 'interest' among the freeholder voters, the gentry made many more. The peerage had much less influence in Hertfordshire politics than in many counties. In 1722 [Table 6A] the clergy vote was: for Sebright 76, Freeman 72, Caesar 16; in 1727 for Sebright 70, Freeman 59 and Caesar 39. Caesar's position had improved at Freeman's expense. The peers can be identified individually. Mrs Caesar noted in her diary: 'Lord Salisbury being against . . . though he had obligations . . . in the Queen's time . . . Lord Essex was also against Mr Caesar.' Plumer wrote to Mrs Caesar on 2 September: 'Lord Essex is working against us at Stortford very warmly, notwithstanding we were in hopes he would have been cool'. Mrs Caesar's diary continued in a way which reveals the conflicts between personal and political loyalties. She explains Essex's opposition as due to a political debt which he owed to Lord Salisbury who had supported Sir William Stanhope when Caesar would not. 'Lord Essex's opposition lasted but till he brought his men into the Town [Hertford, to vote], for he then came to wish me joy of Mr Caesar's being chose by a great majority as it proved.' The Countess of Strafford wrote to Mrs Caesar that she had told Sarah Churchill, Duchess of Marlborough who did not know who stood, that 'Lord Essex and the Duke of Bridgewater was for Sir Thomas and Mr Freeman'. Bridgewater when approached wrote to Caesar: 'I have declared I would not meddle in the next election for Hertfordshire, so hope you will excuse my not serving you', but his tenants supported Sebright, the Duke's neighbour. The Grimstons were against Caesar. William Bucknall wrote from Oxhey on 19 August: 'I am sorry to hear Lord Grimston is engaged; he has great interest'. While Plumer wrote on 22 August of 'a relation Mr Freeman had just made . . . that Lord Grimston would be against you'. He was; oddly enough he had given Caesar a plumper in 1722 but voted SF in 1727.

Sarah Churchill, Duchess of Marlborough's attitude was typical of her unique personality. She told the Countess of Strafford, when 'asked who she was for in Hertfordshire [that] nobody had applied to her nor did she know who stood. So I named the three; she said they were all gentlemen of good estates and they could make a good many votes.' The Countess informed Mary Caesar of this, 'that you may make what use of it you think fit'. Caesar wrote to the Duchess on 18 August and she wrote back two days later: 'till I know who are the candidates for your election, I cannot give a positive answer'. Then followed her statement of political principles already quoted. She went on: 'wherever I have any interest I shall always give it to the best of my knowledge to those gentlemen that have the best characters with a good substance who, I think, will generally be most likely and most capable of serving their country. And, in this way of thinking, I can have no exception to you; but I am really so great a stranger to everything now in Hertfordshire, that I don't know who are your opposers, nor who stands with you. And I should think it a great crime in me ever to be against anybody that is proper to be a representative for any place, if they have been friends to the Duke of Marlborough.' Caesar persisted and Sarah wrote again on 2 September: 'I cannot flatter myself that my interest in Hertfordshire can be of much service to you, I having no estate there but what was my father's at Sandridge'. She felt that she must support Freeman who had always been 'very civil to the Duke . . . and has done us the favour to dine sometimes at Holywell', and had assisted in choosing the last St Albans member. 'But since there must be two chose out of three, it can be no prejudice to you to have those few that I can influence vote for you and Mr Freeman'. In both 1722 and 1727 Caesar got 1 vote in Sandridge, Freeman and Sebright 2. Rather a different Duchess of Marlborough emerges in the letter she wrote on 4 August to Lord Grimston about the St Albans election: 'I have had an account . . . that your lordship and my grandson cannot be chose without spending and bribing to the amount of a thousand pounds . . . therefore I am determined to have no more to do with this election. I think it better to keep the money to help pay the taxes that a single member can't prevent.' So she would leave the field free for Grimston.

The only two peers, who really supported Caesar, had little local influence. Earl Grandison of Queen Hoo in Tewin was a cousin of the Bydes and Harrisons. He wrote, enthusiastically, that he would 'lose no time . . . to make what interest I can to serve you; there are very few freeholders . . . I propose going on purpose to give you my vote'. In Tewin Caesar's vote rose from 9 to 13. Grandison's own vote was cast in Bramfield where the only other voter also plumped for Caesar. Lord Aston, a Roman Catholic, wrote from Standon: 'I have very little time and a more lame interest to serve you, so that the best I can say is that you shall receive no hurt through me'. All the same Caesar's Standon vote went up from 25 in 1722 to 42 in 1727, thirty-seven of which were plumpers, but this may have been as much the work of William Bownest of Hormead, to the north, as of Lord Aston. Plumer reported to Caesar that 'Mr Bownest was . . . serving you very zealously' at Standon on Monday 21 August.[18]

The Active Support of the Local Gentry

Caesar's success was achieved with the help of local gentry. In 1722 122 people, described in the poll books as gentlemen or esquires, voted for Freeman, 112 for Sebright, and only 78 for Caesar. There was a complete reversal in 1727, once again mainly at Freeman's expense: Caesar had 156 votes, Sebright 126, and Freeman only 95

[Table 6B]. The canvassing activities of the more active gentry can be followed in the Caesar correspondence; how they and the local people whose support they won finally voted can be followed in the poll books. Some active opponents can be similarly identified. What happened in four important areas in the county will serve as examples. HITCHIN, OFFLEY and KING'S WALDEN were all solid for Caesar. *Hitchin* was managed by the two grandsons of the Sir Ralph Radcliffe who had fought the County as a Whig in 1715. Edward, the dynamic younger brother wrote from London about 25 August: 'My brother [Ralph] is returned . . . and approves of the steps I have taken to promote your interest, and adds he shall be at Hitchin tomorrow or on Saturday at furthest, in order to leave no stone unturned that may be of service to you . . . My brother believes it may be of use to you that you make Hitchin a visit . . . he believes . . . Wednesday following [the 30th], if you approve of it, as in the country conveniency for provisions must be considered, he designing to give an entertainment to the Freeholders, at dinner'. So Caesar was asked to let the Radcliffes know, in time, whether he could come. Ralph added a PS: 'Sir I am so much tired I can only assure you I will do you all the service that lies in my power'. The final Hitchin vote was most satisfactory for Caesar: the SF vote fell from 22 to 6 and the C vote rose from 48 to 116; Freeman lost 27 of the FC votes which he had had in 1722.

Neighbouring *Offley* was the estate of Sir Henry Penrice, an admiralty court judge. His wife, Elizabeth, daughter of Sir Humphrey Gore of Gilston and Elizabeth Spencer, had brought Penrice this one time Spencer property. Plumer wrote on 23 August: 'Mr Byde set out this morning . . . I hope you take care of Sir Henry Penrice'; and Richard, Plumer's brother, wrote on 5 September: 'Sir Henry Penrice, not caring to come to Hertford is gone to Gloucester election, but the town of Offley stand well engaged as Mr Byde left them, and there was no ground for any suspicion of Sir Henry's endeavouring to alter them'. The suspicion had been voiced in a letter to Mary Caesar from Robinson Lytton of Knebworth who played a key part in Caesar's victory as we have seen: 'I fell into company last night that assured me Sir Henry Penrice had taken grub at something and become our enemy'. 'Grub' in contemporary English meant 'sulky or bad tempered' [OED]. Penrice who had voted C in 1722 did not vote in Offley in 1727 though the Offley voters remained faithful to Caesar: his vote rose from 24 to 27, Freeman's fell from 9 to 2, while Sebright's rose from 7 to 8.

King's Walden, south of Offley, was Plumer's concern. It was the home of the Hales. The heirs in 1727 were minors, their uncles their guardians. Sir Bernard Hale, baron of the Exchequer and the most distinguished of the uncles, was also William Plumer's uncle. His sister was Plumer's mother. Plumer wrote that on Monday 28 he would 'see

Baron Hale who sets out for Kings Walden the next day . . . to concert with him how to manage those people'. On Tuesday 29 Plumer wrote: 'I have seen my uncle Hale who is this day set out for his brother's at King's Walden and I hope that matter is set right'.[19] King's Walden voted very satisfactorily for Caesar, giving him 29 votes to Sebright's 5, with none for Freeman.

The second area, in the north-east of the county – ROYSTON, BUNTINGFORD, THERFIELD, WYDDIAL and HORMEAD – was in Freeman influenced territory. Caesar's most active and successful supporter here was Richard Goulston of Wyddial, an old Tory and Caesar's running mate in Hertford Borough elections since 1701. The Goulston – Caesar alliance was older even than this, for a Royalist plotter interrogated by the Commonwealth government in 1651 had confessed, 'There is one Squire Caesar, Mr Gulston . . . and others . . . will be ready to assist in those parts . . . at Royston'.[20] Goulston had voted SF in 1722 but he voted C in 1727. His advocacy must have been a major factor in Caesar's advance in the north-east. He was an inveterate optimist and a combative canvasser. On 20 August he wrote: 'Were all places like my neighbourhood at *Buntingford,* little hesitation should determine for you . . . you shall know what I have done . . . I went yesterday to the aforesaid town to enquire into the dispositions of the mortals of that place, and in short found all I could wish . . . *Royston* I have good reason to know are more than ever in your interest and Captain Crouch has had such smartness with Robin Chester that the old Esquire's nose will receive very ill treatment should he be again impertinent. Indeed he's a brute and as such should be used. I have this day had some small warmth with my parson, Heton, who does not directly deny me, but desires he may have a small time to consider of the point.' On 27 August Goulston reported that he had been back to Royston where 'I had great success . . . and nowhere fail of great encouragement. I attacked *Hormead* yesterday where, though an invenomed Divine, nay the most unmannerly so I have yet met with, had engaged most of them, I broke through his measures and have reclaimed a good half. *Therfield* claims regard and I have been sent to, but am in wood what to do.'[21] 'In wood' meant 'at a loss, in perplexity' [OED].

In Royston, Buntingford and Therfield the voting changed in the same way: Sebright's vote fell, Freeman's fell a little, and Caesar's rose to become the biggest vote. In Wyddial Sebright and Freeman lost all their votes and Caesar doubled his. In Royston Robert Chester voted SF in 1722 and 1727. In Wyddial Richard and Francis Goulston, Richard's son, had voted SF in 1722, as had the Reverend Thomas Heton. Richard Goulston voted C in 1727, while Heton voted FC but in Buntingford. In 1722 Charles Crouch had voted C in Buntingford, for a Wyddial property; in 1727 Joseph Crouch voted C in Weston. Only in the Hormeads did Goulston fail; though Freeman's and Sebright's votes fell slightly, Freeman still had nearly twice as many votes in 1727 as Caesar. The Reverend Thomas Doe who voted SF in 1722 and 1727 must have been the 'invenomed divine' of Goulston's letter. He had more effective local influence than Goulston or William Bownest, lord of the manor of Stonebury in Little Hormead. Although Bownest voted, in Hormead, FC in 1722, C in 1727, his effective canvassing was in Standon.

Plumer and his immediate associates were effectively active in a third area, a group of parishes in the south-east of the county – STANDON, the HADHAMS, BISHOPS STORTFORD, and SAWBRIDGEWORTH. *Standon* swung to Caesar 25 : 42, while Freeman's vote fell 45 : 28 and Sebright's 31 : 21. This was Lord Aston's parish, though Bownest was the effective canvasser. In the *Hadhams,* east of Standon, Caesar had already had a majority in 1722, which was substantially increased in 1727, 25 : 36. William Stanley, Dean of St Asaph's and Canon of St Paul's was Rector of Much Hadham. Plumer wrote that on Friday 18 August 'two of the Mr Stanleys, Peter and Felix Calvert dined with me . . . and will serve you what they can; and Dean Stanley will lie still'. On 22 August Plumer wrote again: 'at Hadham I believe by the help of Felix Calvert and Mr Stanley you will do very well'. On 24 August Plumer reported 'your new allies Felix and Peter Calvert and Mr Stanley take true and hearty pains and with success'. William Stanley DD voted SF in 1722; William Stanley esquire and the Revd Francis Stanley voted C in 1727. Felix Calvert voted SF in 1722 and C in 1727 in the Pelhams. Peter Calvert voted in Hunsdon. Two other Calverts, another Felix in Albury and William in the Pelhams, voted SF in 1722 and 1727. The very large increase in Caesar's *Stortford* vote, 37 to 60, with a small drop in Freeman's and Sebright's votes, both under 40, was a considerable tribute to Plumer's personal electioneering. When he wrote, on 23 August, he was not over optimistic; he preferred to underestimate Caesar's support: 'I went early this morning to Stortford where I think we may depend upon a good half of the people. My friends say more, but I love to underreckon. I saw most of them myself and left instructions for those who were out of the way to be applied to, and will have a guard upon them for they are hard beset by Mr Sandford and the clergy.' John Sandford and the Reverend John Took voted SF in 1722 and 1727, as did the Reverend Robert Stileman in 1727. Three other, new, gentry voters were Caesar plumpers; one came from Essex. Some of Caesar's improved vote may have been produced by 'the men of interest in Essex upon the borders [who Plumer met when stag hunting]. I hope we shall have their help with some outliers.' In *Sawbridgeworth,* where there was a much more radical reversal of voting than in Stortford, the indirect influence may have been Dr Richard Mead. Mead was a leading London physician, a Whig who moved in the highest political and cultural circles, but who had used his influence with Walpole to free the Tory Dr John Freind from the Tower where he was imprisoned in 1723 under suspicion of involvement in the Atterbury plot. On 2 September Dr Richard Mead wrote to Caesar: 'I have found out Mr Hanchet and pressed him as much as possible in your favour'.[22] Hanchet voted in Sawbridgeworth, FC in 1722; though he did not vote in 1727 his influence may have helped Caesar whose votes rose 28 : 48, while Freeman's fell 61 : 37 and Sebright's 50 : 28. The 'men of interest in Essex' helped. In 1727 Caesar had voting support, in Sawbridgeworth, from two London and three Essex gentry.

Electioneering in WARE and to the south in AMWELL, STANSTEAD, HODDESDON, BROXBOURNE, WORMLEY and CHESHUNT, was particularly intense. Plumer's hope for *Amwell* was the Reverend Mr Kent, Rector of Netteswell in Essex; 'he votes for Amwell'. In Amwell, while Caesar's vote dropped 19 : 17, Freeman's and Sebright's smaller votes fell even more. Kent had voted SF in 1722 but did not vote in 1727, though a Dr Clarke voted C. In *Stanstead,* south-east of Ware, the votes for all three candidates also fell but Caesar's only slightly; while Caesar had 21 votes, all plumpers, there was a single SF vote only. John Byde's and Plumer's electoral forecasts were surprisingly accurate. Byde wrote on 29 August of 'about twenty-six [freeholders] engaging themselves for single votes'; and Plumer had written six days earlier: 'We hope . . . we shall have the town single Caesar'. The local manor belonged to the Feilde family who also held the advowson. The Feildes were John Byde's cousins. George Harrison of Balls Park married Mr Feilde's sister. Plumer hoped 'Mr Field will at least acquiesce'.[23] He did not vote but the vicar, the Reverend Robert Audleybritten, voted C in 1727, as did John Byde whose house, Bonningtons, was in the parish.

In *Hoddesdon* 'Mr Rawdon . . . should be thought of'. Marmaduke Roydon voted C in 1722 and 1727. All three candidates' votes rose, but Freeman's and Sebright's more than Caesar's. The votes were Freeman 12 : 18; Sebright 11 : 14; and Caesar 14 : 16. In *Broxbourne* Caesar's vote rose 3 : 4, while Freeman's fell 5 : 2 and Sebright's also fell 4 : 1. Sir John Monson was lord of the manor of Broxbourne. Plumer wrote 'his name will be an assistance'. John Byde reported that Monson had 'sent a letter to his bailiff, recommending [Caesar's] interest single'. The bailiff went to Stanstead to see Byde who 'wrote out for him a list of the voters in Cheshunt, Broxbourne and Hoddesdon which I found he wanted'. In *Wormley* voting moved, marginally, against Caesar: Caesar 2 : 2; SF 3 : 4. In *Cheshunt* the faithful Daniel Dodson, whom Plumer mentioned in his letters, voted C as he had in 1722. Overall Caesar's large majority continued 37 : 36 to Sebright's 9 : 19 and Freeman's 8 : 16. The doubling of the SF vote from 8 to 16 was due to William Shaw and Samuel Robinson. Byde had warned that 'Mr Shaw of Theobalds I fear will a little break in upon Sir John Monson's interest'; and Plumer: 'I find Sir John Monson's letter has done service in securing some and confirming others that doubted. Mr Shaw and Samuel Robinson are against you.' Of the eleven gentry and clerical voters in Cheshunt, seven voted SF.

In *Ware* the huge Caesar vote which increased 85 : 118, and the loss of votes by his opponents – Freeman 51 : 27 and Sebright 32 : 17 – was hardly surprising. This was Plumer's own territory. Though his father-in-law, Thomas Byde, did oppose, it was in vain. Plumer 'spent some hours at Ware market [on the 22nd] and find my kinsman Byde is very vigorous against you'.[24] Seven of eight London gentry, two of them Stanleys, who voted in Ware gave Caesar plumpers.

Canvassing

How the local gentry made an interest, won and held the support of electors, emerges from the Caesar correspondence. There was real canvassing; Goulston's was particularly vigorous. There were 'bribes', voters were rewarded in kind and, sometimes, in cash. In 1727 Goulston 'bespoke at two houses [inns] what I think proper to keep . . . hearts warm for my friend's service'; Bucknall was 'now drinking your success with some of your voters'. John Byde was surrounded by all the 'freeholders of Stanstead . . . drinking to your success'. As we have seen, the Radcliffes designed 'an entertainment to the freeholders, at dinner'. Plumer wrote that in Bishops Stortford the 'candidates of the other side, having contributed to a new organ are become very dear to the Church'. In 1734 Frances Harcourt wrote to Mrs Caesar: 'there will be about thirty people that will not go, unless they can be certain of ten shillings a man for their journey'. If Caesar will not pay 'they will take the money for the other side. I will be bound that every man that has the money shall vote for Mr Caesar; and they that give a vote for Mr Caesar and one of the others shall have but a Crown apiece. There are a great many that expect nothing, but these that want the money are only poor labouring men.'[25] There was nothing exceptional about this; similar sums were paid in Hertford Borough in the 1830s; more shocking was the St Albans Borough election bribery in 1722 when 'upwards of 150' voters were bribed with sums like ten, fifteen, and eighteen guineas, for which receipts were given. 'Received, March 14th, 1721/2, of Thomas Gape, esquire, ten pounds ten shillings, upon consideration that I am to vote for William Gore and William Clayton, esquires, at the next election of burgesses in parliament for the borough of St Albans, and I do promise to repay the same again if I do not vote as aforesaid. Witness my hand.' No wonder the Duchess of Marlborough withdrew from the 1727 St Albans election because of the expense.[26]

The country gentry used their tenants and bailiffs to canvass other tenants, whose votes, however, were for their own freeholds *not* for leased property. Sarah Churchill sent Caesar 'a letter to that tenant which I think most capable of speaking to the rest; and you will be pleased to send your own messenger with it, if you think it will be of any service to you'. John Byde wrote that 'Sir John Monson has sent a letter to his Bailiff recommending your interest single'. Plumer advised using 'some good agent' in Dacorum. Circular letters were sent: 'I will disperse your circular letters as I find occasion but believe you will send to our neighbouring gentlemen yourself'; and 'I am desired to let you know a letter to the Revd Mr Kent, rector of Netteswell in Essex, will gain him for you. I do not answer for this but, if you please, my servant that brings this shall carry one to him; possibly if a common circular letter is meant, he may have had one; he votes for Amwell.'[27]

Caesar published an electoral broadsheet, entitled *The Harford Election*, with a cut of himself in a circle, surrounded by Britannia on the left, and pastoral, sea and town scenes on the right. The verses were appalling, and unbelievably trite:[28]

'Come all you noble hearts of Gold
You that are all freeholders
Your Vote and Interest let us have
For Caeser there nere was a bolder
No in the County of Harfordshire
Try him and then you'll see sir
You never will Repent the time
You gave your Vote for Caeser.

'His temper is generous and free
And will stand by his Country
And Nobly his great Estate
You know he spent amongst ye
Therefore my boys in gratetude
Ne're vallue whose displeas'd sir
You never can Repent, etc.

'No Bribs at all he e're will give
His Interest for to make sir
Tread he frely would retrieve
Which long has lain at stake sir
His Countreys good he has at heart
As you may plainly see sir
I'm sure you never can Repent
You gave, etc.

'The poor he never yet did Scorn
Nor Charity deny'd them
When at his Gates they ere did call
He frely did supply them
Besides he loves the church my Boys
We're sure he is no Rumper
So heres to Caeser heart and Voice
Each man toss off a Bumper

'And wish him in the house to set
For three years and no longer
And then again if we think fit
That he shall then return sir
For seven years it is to long
For to stay of an Arrant
Besids it does the Country wrong
So we will have no more ont.

'So to conclude my merry Boys
Toss off your Glass to Caeser
And merrely we will rejoyce
In hopes he will have the day sir
Because he is Loyal just and true
We hope he will it attaine sir
See you that Loves your Countrys Good
Pray give your Vote for Caeser.'
[spelling as in original]

The Spider's Web

In some ways the most fascinating aspect of the group of people who really decided the parliamentary representation of Hertfordshire in the middle of the eighteenth century is the network of marriage relationships. Plumer's friend, Mr Roper, was active in assisting Caesar's campaign. On 27 August Plumer wrote: 'Mr Roper . . . has an account from Mr Lomax, his cousin, that he goes on very prosperously at St Albans'. This was Caleb Lomax who won a St Albans Borough seat in 1727. He voted C in 1727, as had his father, Joshua, in 1722 when Joshua had been defeated in the borough election by William Gore. Gore voted in Tring, SF in 1722 and 1727; he was to support Caesar in 1734. Gore's daughter was married to Richard Mead, son of the Dr Mead who supported Caesar. Charles Caesar was, of course, Ralph Freeman's brother-in-law. Ralph's sister, Elizabeth, married Robert Elwes whose son, another Robert, married Martha Cary, sister of the Jane Cary who married Henry Long of Bayford. Their daughter, Jane, married Charles and Mary Caesar's son, the younger Charles. Hence the references to Cary and Elwes when Caesar was dealing with 'Miss' Long's inheritance. William Hale, grandfather of William Plumer and father of Sir Bernard Hale, had married a Mary Elwes, who was the aunt of the Robert Elwes who married Elizabeth Freeman.

This is complicated enough, but when the family network is looked at from the standpoint of William Plumer the complexity is mind bog-gling. William Plumer of Blakesware was the centre of an immense family network deeply involved in Hertfordshire politics in the 1720s and later. Two Hale uncles, Sir Bernard and Jeremiah, and Nicholas Bonfoy, aunt Hale's husband, have appeared in the electioneering. So have Plumer's brother, Richard, and brother-in-law, Thomas Byde, Thomas' cousins, John Byde, Mr (Paul or William) Feilde, and their sister Mary Feilde's husband, George Harrison. George was the broth-er of Edward, 'Governor' Harrison. The Harrisons' sister, Elizabeth, married Edward Hughes who, on 26 September 1727, congratulated Caesar on his election, in glowing terms: 'your generosity, humanity, and benevolence, which has gained you the love of mankind, . . . as it expresses the long hid character of him, you have defeated'.[29] John, Earl Grandison was a cousin of the Harrisons and of Thomas Byde. A family tree, to illustrate this, would stretch across two or three pages. The importance is not in the detail but in the appreciation that this was an age when family links were still strong and family connexions used to promote individual interests.

William Plumer was the spider at the centre of this web. He was like a spider in another respect, like the female black widow. He worked hard to destroy, politically, the deeply entrenched Hanoverian Tory county member, Ralph Freeman, using the Jacobite Charles Caesar as his instrument. Having succeeded he, then, consumed Caesar. What Freeman thought of the behaviour of Plumer and his friends in 1727 is revealed in the *Diary of the first Earl of Egmont*:

'After dinner I went to the Crown Tavern to a public concert . . . I met there Mr Freeman, an old gentleman who had been knight of the shire for Hertfordshire thirty years, but lost his election in the first Parliament of his present Majesty by means of Sir Robert Walpole.

'He told me that when the king came to the Crown His Majesty sent to him and told him he hoped that as he had always shown himself a friend to his family, he would be in the House in this first Parliament of his reign. Mr Freeman replied he did not think of standing, but if His Majesty thought it for his service, he would, but then he hoped His Majesty's servants would not oppose him. The King replied they should on the contrary assist him. So down he went, but when the election came on he found the Government's officers oppose him to a man in favour of Mr Caesar, a much higher Tory than himself . . . whom the Jacobites now supported. Surprised at this, he caused those officers to be spoke to, who replied they dared not do otherwise, for it might cost them their employments. In a word, Mr Freeman lost the election, and being returned to London he acquainted the King how he had been served. The King was very angry with Sir Robert.

'As he came out of His Majesty's closet he met Sir Robert going in, who, stopping him, expressed his surprise that he had not carried his election, asked him how it was possible, and declared nothing had surprised and vexed him more. Mr Freeman replied, "Don't ask me how I lost it, you know that better than I", at which Sir Robert blushed up to his eyes, which, said Mr Freeman, is the only time I ever saw him blush.'[30]

The Disaster in 1734: Plumer defeats Caesar

Plumer achieved his ultimate objective and Freeman got his revenge in 1734. Plumer stood himself in the general election on 2 May. As early as 1 October 1733 a meeting had been held 'to fix on two persons to be recommended to the electors to represent the County' at the next general election. At this meeting Freeman's son proposed Sir Thomas Sebright and Caesar's former Whig ally, William Plumer. The proposal 'met with universal compliance excepting Mr [Charles] Gore, who spoke for some time in commendation of Mr Caesar's behaviour in Parliament and thought it strange that he should be so unanimously dropped'.[31]

Mary Caesar's comment in her diary was typical of her loyalty and her vivid use of language: 'Mr Caesar in the many stages of his various changes in life fell among a set of disputatious robbers. Not a chance traveller, but his friend, his neighbour, went secretly to many saying come now help me strip him of his feather; and after many private came to a public meeting there to declare it. Where Mr Gore's behaviour to Mr Caesar was such that from the family he justly merits the title of the good Samaritan.' 'W Plumer, Knight of the Shire' was written in the margin against this comment.[32] William Gore, Charles' father, who had voted SF in 1722 and 1727, wrote to Caesar on 12 April 1734 expressing his disgust with the underhand proceedings. Caesar was unsure as to whether to stand; he was deeply in debt. In one letter which he wrote in April, possibly to William Gore, he referred, obliquely, to the way his financial situation was being exploited by his opponents: 'I am very much pleased to hear that my opponents' chief dependence now is upon my not appearing in person at the election, nor having a sufficient qualification, in both of which points they will find themselves very much mistaken'.[33] Caesar kept up an optimistic front: 'I have very great reason to believe that through the assistance of my friends I shall carry the election by as great a majority as I did last time'.[34] Without the Plumer – Whig election machine this proved a false hope. There were 72 fewer votes cast than in 1727, but 295 more than in 1722. Caesar was humiliated. Plumer headed the poll with 2197 votes, more than Caesar had received in 1727. Sebright, the eternal survivor, came second with 1842, an increase on his earlier votes. Caesar had a mere 1187, fewer even than the 1340 which he had received in 1722.

In almost every area in which Caesar had triumphed in 1727 he met disaster in 1734. In every Hundred in the County his votes were well below those of 1727 [Table 2]; in the eighteen most populated places in the county [Table 5] he had fewer votes than in 1722. In Hertford, Hitchin, Stortford, Watford and Ware Caesar lost votes massively. The only urban areas in which he gained votes were in Baldock, Berkhamsted and Tring. These last two may have been due to the help of John Trott junior who wrote from Berkhamsted on 2 April: 'I gave two barrels of beer to the freeholders and populace and had all their inclinations for you'.[35] Even so Plumer and Sebright had more votes than Caesar in Berkhamsted, though not in Tring where, perhaps, Gore's help was effective. The most devastating defeat for Caesar came in the area he had so successfully controlled in 1722 and 1727 [Table 3E]. In these thirty-five places he had fewer votes in 1734 than either of the victorious candidates: 388 to Sebright's 440 and Plumer's 640. Plumer topped the poll in sixteen small and medium-sized places in this area *and* in Cheshunt with 40 votes, Hertford with 55, Hitchin with 99 and Ware with 111. Caesar came first in only eighteen places, but only six of these gave him more than 15 votes. Benington, his home, gave him 32 votes to Plumer's 6 and Sebright's 2; the Mundens gave him 28 votes to Plumer's 15 and Sebright's 4; Welwyn gave him 27 votes to Plumer's 13 and Sebright's 4.

Ironically Caesar's vote was firmest in Freeman's area. He had almost doubled his vote between 1722 and 1727 and only dropped five votes in 1734. Sebright dropped eight but still had more than twice as many votes as Caesar. Plumer easily headed the poll in this area, actually polling five more votes than Freeman had in 1727 [Table 3D].

Lytton remained faithful to Caesar. Graveley, Knebworth and Stevenage gave Caesar 81 votes, 67 of which were plumpers, to only 30 for Plumer and 18 for Sebright [Table 3C]. Lytton had written on 30 March, too optimistically, that Caesar had the general voice with not less than 200 votes from Hitchin and Stevenage alone. In the event they gave Caesar only 112 to Plumer's 124 and Sebright's 91. Caesar had support in the east of the County from John Ives of Stanstead, W Benn of Westmill and a relative, E Elwes. However the only places, among the ten or so his friends mentioned, in which Caesar did even reasonably well were Buntingford and Royston. Ives' list of six people whom 'I am sure will not only vote for you, but have a very good interest' was particularly misguided.[36] In the four places he listed Caesar got 37 votes, Plumer 210! There is an obscure reference in an earlier letter from Joshua Goulston which may explain some of Caesar's loss of support, *if* it refers to the 'betrayal' of Freeman in 1727: 'You cannot safely imagine the distaste this new alteration[?] has made amongst the farmerly freeholders, and very [likely?] they accuse your very person who was the first contriver of this change'.[37] Plumer's 1734 campaign seems to have been a mirror image of Caesar's in 1727: attack Caesar on his home ground and do a deal with Sebright. We have no correspondence to confirm this. However Sebright secured himself by an even closer voting alliance with Plumer than he had had with Freeman in 1722 or Caesar in 1727. The total joint SP vote in 1734 was 1676; in 1722 Sebright had had 190 votes in addition to the SF vote; in 1727 602, of which 346 were SC votes; in 1734 Sebright had only 166 votes in addition to the SP vote. In his own area [Table 3A] Sebright had only 16 votes more than Plumer. He had only 24 plumpers as compared with 183 in 1727 and 83 in 1722. Sebright's joint vote with Caesar in this area fell from 103 to 36 and Caesar's overall vote from 194 to 112.

The Hand of Providence: Caesar's reelection

The Whig triumph and Caesar's humiliation seemed complete in 1734 but Caesar was to find unexpected friends. In April 1736 there was a by-election for the County on Sir Thomas Sebright's death. Mrs Caesar describes what happened in her own inimitable way: 'Upon the death of Sir Thomas Sebright, Mr Caesar's opposers had set Mr Halsey up, to have been chose as they thought on the Thursday [22 April, polling day], but the Saturday before at the Hertford Club Mr Caesar's friends without his knowledge, or so much as any previous thought of theirs, resolved to publish that for him they would demand a poll, which they carried; and when Mr Dean, as sheriff, declared him many said: "This is the hand of Providence".' The poll was very close and low: Caesar 1078, Henshaw Halsey 1019. Interestingly Caesar had written in 1734 to win William Gore's support: 'I am morally sure that those who now oppose me never intend to set you up for the County; in one case Bucknall will be their man, in another Sebright again, or Halsey'. Mrs Caesar's diary continues: 'twas . . . Mr Harrison who in the field demanded the poll, seconded by Dr Clark, thirded by Mr Benn of Westmill who so vastly assisted in London and country. They forced him [Benn] into the chair, there to be carried to represent Mr Caesar'. Caesar was in a debtors' gaol from which his election released him. Mrs Caesar wrote in the margin: 'when Mr Caesar went down all was renewed'. This was against her revealing description of the rejoicing: 'I'm told the rejoicings were beyond imagination, not only at Hertford, the fountain head, but in all the towns, and though Mr William Plumer against him Ware was illumined to the very stumps that cross the street.

'The morning the news reached London Lord Grimston came to tell me how glad he was to hear St Albans had behaved so well, but said he did not wonder at it, for Mr Caesar had there a personal interest himself. He complained, as did the Duke of Leeds [Thomas Osborne] and many others of not having had notice . . Lord Essex coming, after leaving Turin, said for a country [election] there never was anything like it before in the world.'[38] In 1734 Essex had supported Plumer and Sebright!

The election of an absentee bankrupt with only five days of possible electioneering was remarkable and is some tribute to Caesar's personal qualities. His friendships probably played a bigger part in his election successes than conventional political analyses allow for. Caesar died in 1741, just before the general election, 'at which Charles Gore and Jacob Houblon, both Tories, were returned without a contest. In 1747 Gore, who by this time had gone over to the Government, was re-elected and Houblon was replaced by Paggen Hale, a government supporter, without opposition.'[39] Paggen Hale was William Plumer's cousin once removed. The scene was set for the triumph of the cousinry in county representation over the next sixty years. As surname or christian name Plumer, Byde and Hale recur again and again in Hertfordshire politics in the eighteenth and early nineteenth centuries. While some of the MPs who represented the County or the two Boroughs were government supporters, the remarkable fact is the survival of a strong anti-establishment tradition. 'All the six MPs from Hertfordshire voted for the no-confidence motion which ended Lord North's government in 1782, for the censure motion which broke the younger Pitt in 1806, and for the Reform Bill in 1832. William Plumer of Blakesware, son of Caesar's Judas-like "election agent", represented the County for thirty-nine years from 1768 to 1807. He was one of the small band of Whigs who remained faithful to Charles James Fox as national hysteria mounted during the war against revolutionary France. In his regular role as Teller for the Opposition motions against the war or wartime repression and for parliamentary and other reforms, he was a more consistent heir to Charles Caesar, the Jacobite, than might appear at first sight.'[40]

NOTES

1   Letterbook B, Nos 11 & 17

2   Letterbooks D, No 14 and A, No 25

3   Letterbooks A, No 24 & B, No 32; *HMC Report on Manuscripts of the Earl of Verulam.* 1906, pp 117-9; H F C Lansberry 'A Whig Inheritance' in *Bulletin of the Institute of Historical Research* Vol XLI, (May 1968) p 47

4   J H Plumb *Sir Robert Walpole: the King's Minister.* (1960) p 98 & note

5   Letterbook A, No 23

6   Mary Caesar's diary, BL. Add. Ms. 62558; Letterbook B, No 5

7   Letterbooks B, No 24; A, No 26; B, No 29; A, No 27. HCRO D/EP F 53. HCRO has printed poll books for 1727, QPE 13; and for 1734, QPE 21; there is a Ms. poll book for 1722, QPE 6-12.

8   Letterbooks B, Nos 8, 12, 18, 23, 27 & 29; E, No 19; B, No 34

9   *The Life, Letters and Literary Remains of Edward Bulwer, Lord Lytton* by his son. (1883) Vol. 1, pp 43-4

10 Letterbook B, Nos 9, 12, 13, 14 & 15

11 Letterbook B, Nos 16, 18 & 19

12 *HMC 15th Rep. Mss. of the Duke of Portland.* Appendix Part IV. 1897, p 154. Quoted in *VCH. of Hertfordshire* Vol 2. (1908) p 40

13 Plumb, *op. cit.* p 98. This is particularly embarrassing because, in a note, Sir John quoted an unpublished article of mine as evidence; the text of this article did NOT support Sir John's statement.

14 Letterbook B, Nos 16 & 18

15 Mr W Brown of Hatfield lent me this letter which was, I believe, in The Fryth, Welwyn.

16 Letterbook B, No 16; *DNB* Vol XLIII, p 402, Compact Edition, p 1601; *Madingley Hall, a Short History and Description,* Lionel M Munby (1961)

17 Letterbook B, Nos 26, 20, 23 & 29

18 Diary, *op. cit.*; Letterbooks E, Nos 19 & 17; B, Nos 30, 11, 16, 14 & 32; *Verulam,* op. cit. p 121; Letterbook B, Nos 28, 21 & 16

19 Letterbooks B, Nos 20, 18 & 33; E, No 20; B, Nos 26 & 23. For the

Radcliffes see Ralph Davis *Aleppo and Devonshire Square.* (1967); and Reginald L Hine *The History of Hitchin.* 2 vols. (1927 & 1929) *en passim*

20 *HMC 13th Rep. Part 1. Mss. of the Duke of Portland* Vol I. 1891, p 581

21 Letterbook B, Nos 13 & 25

22 Letterbook B, Nos 16, 12, 19, 18 & 31

23 Letterbook B, Nos 23 & 27

24 Letterbook B, Nos 19, 23, 27, 29 & 16

25 Letterbook B, Nos 13, 17, 27, 20 &18; G dated 28 April 1734

26 *Verulam,* op. cit. p 119

27 Letterbook B, Nos 32, 27, 19, 16 & 22

28 Letterbook B, No 37

29 Letterbook B, Nos 26 & 35

30 *HMC. Mss. of the Earl of Egmont.* Diary Vol II. 1734-8 3(1923) pp 164-5

31 *History of Parliament*, op. cit., pp 260-1

32 Diary, *op. cit.*

33 Letterbook C, No 28

34 Letterbook C, No 28

35 Letterbook C, No 25

36 Letterbook C, Nos 24, 19, 20, 21 & 30 and G letter of 28 April

37 Letterbook C, No 18

38 Diary, *op. cit.*; Letterbook C, No 28

39 *History of Parliament*, op. cit., p 261

40 Lionel M Munby 'Politics and Religion in Hertfordshire 1660-1740' *East Anglian Studies.* (1968) p 142

Table 1. VOTING BY LONDON RESIDENTS IN 1722 AND 1727

	CAESAR				FREEMAN				SEBRIGHT			
	C	FC	SC	Total	F	FC	FS	Total	S	SC	SF	Total
1722	88	24	8	= 120	0	24	82	= 106	7	8	82	= 97
1727	125	7	21	= 153	1	7	43	= 51	6	21	43	= 70

Table 2. HOW VOTING WAS DISTRIBUTED IN EACH HUNDRED
(MAP A)

HUNDRED	1722			1727			1734		
	C	S	F	C	S	F	C	S	P
Odsey	97	102	124	123	97	122	98	102	132
Edwinstree	78	126	159	133	125	157	76	162	197
Braughing	255	221	278	358	143	192	110	344	469
Hertford	189	56	74	206	69	68	115	120	196
Broadwater	244	199	226	356	143	134	308	121	191
Hitchin	178	96	128	277	101	21	105	191	228
Dacorum	101	402	339	254	428	153	174	449	414
Cashio	195	227	252	314	318	165	201	353	370
Total	1341	1462	1609	2021	1424	1012	1187	1842	2197

C = votes for Caesar
S = votes for Sebright
F = votes for Freeman
P = votes for Plumer

The figures for 1722 come from the manuscript poll book. The officially accepted totals which I have used in my text were slightly different:

Caesar : 1340   Sebright : 1464   Freeman : 1614

Table 3A. DISTRIBUTION OF VOTES IN THE AREA IN WHICH SEBRIGHT HAD THE HIGHEST VOTE IN 1722 AND IN 1727 (MAP B)

Year	CAESAR				SEBRIGHT				FREEMAN/PLUMER			
	C	CS	CF/P	Total	S	SC	SF/P	Total	F/P	FC/PC	SF/SP	Total
1722	57	6	13	= 76	83	6	235	= 324	1	13	235	= 249
1727	89	103	2	= 194	183	103	87	= 373	1	2	87	= 90
1734	55	36	27	= 118	24	36	317	= 377	12	27	317	= 356
				(112)				(349)				(333)

This covers the following 14 almost contiguous places, in which Sebright had the highest votes: Berkhamsted, Caddington, Flamstead, both Gaddesdens, Harpenden, Hemel Hempstead, Hexton, Kensworth, both Langleys, Lilley, Redbourn and Tring. The detailed 1734 figures cover 15 places; the totals in brackets are for the same 14 places as the 1722 and 1727 figures.

Table 3B. DISTRIBUTION OF VOTES IN THE ST ALBANS AREA (MAP B)

Year	CAESAR				SEBRIGHT				FREEMAN/PLUMER			
	C	CS	CF/P	Total	S	SC	SF/P	Total	F/P	FC/PC	SF/SP	Total
1722	62	6	16	= 84	2	6	97	= 105	0	16	97	= 113
1727	70	58	1	= 129	13	58	57	= 128	0	1	57	= 58
1734	41	36	18	= 95	1	18	105	= 124	2	36	105	= 143

This includes St Albans, St Michaels, St Peters & St Stephens.

Table 3C. DISTRIBUTION OF VOTES IN LYTTON'S HOME TERRITORY (MAP B)

Year	CAESAR				SEBRIGHT				FREEMAN/PLUMER			
	C	CS	CF/P	Total	S	SC	SF/P	Total	F/P	FC/PC	SF/SP	Total
1722	22	14	5	= 41	0	14	53	= 67	1	5	53	= 59
1727	83	11	1	= 95	1	11	6	= 18	0	1	6	= 7
1734	67	2	12	= 81	0	2	16	= 18	2	12	16	= 30

This covers the following three parishes, in which Lytton controlled the voting: Graveley, Knebworth, Stevenage.

Table 3D. DISTRIBUTION OF VOTES IN THE AREA IN WHICH FREEMAN HAD THE HIGHEST VOTE IN 1722 AND 1727
(MAP B)

Year	CAESAR				SEBRIGHT				FREEMAN/PLUMER			
	C	CS	CF/P	Total	S	SC	SF/P	Total	F/P	FC/PC	SF/SP	Total
1722	23	3	30	= 56	1	3	216	= 220	77	30	216	= 253
1727	76	3	30	= 109	1	3	223	= 227	9	30	223	= 262
1734	60	5	39	= 104	0	5	214	= 219	14	39	214	= 267

This covers the following 21 contiguous places in which Freeman had the highest votes: Albury, Aspenden, Baldock, Barkway, Barley, Braughing, Buckland, Bygrave, Clothall, Cottered, Hinxworth, both Hormeads, Kelshall, Meesden, 3 Pelhams, Sandon, Wallington, Westmill.

Table 3E. DISTRIBUTION OF VOTES IN THE AREA IN WHICH CAESAR HAD THE HIGHEST VOTE IN 1722 AND 1727
(MAP B)

Year	CAESAR				SEBRIGHT				FREEMAN/PLUMER			
	C	CS	CF/P	Total	S	SC	SF/P	Total	F/P	FC/PC	SF/SP	Total
1722	526	31	130	= 687	5	31	151	= 187	6	130	151	= 287
1727	730	73	48	= 851	19	73	81	= 173	10	48	81	= 139
1734	249	13	157	= 419	1	13	435	= 449	61	157	435	= 653
				(388)				(440)				(640)

This covers the following 35 almost contiguous places in which Caesar had the highest votes: 2 Amwells, Ardeley, Aston, Bayford, Benington, Bengeo, Cheshunt, Datchworth, Digswell, Eastwick, Gilston, 2 Hadhams, Hertford, Hertingfordbury, Hitchin, Hunsdon, Ippollitts, Kimpton, 2 Mundens, Offley, Sacomb, Stanstead, Tewin, 2 Waldens, Walkern, Ware, Watton, Welwyn, Weston, Widford, 2 Wymondleys. The detailed 1734 figures cover 40 places; the totals in brackets are for the same 35 places as the 1722 and 1727 figures.

Table 4. QUAKER VOTES IN 1722 AND 1727

Year	CAESAR				FREEMAN				SEBRIGHT			
	C	FC	SC	Total	F	FC	FS	Total	S	SC	SF	Total
1722	16	41	1	= 58	4	41	6	= 51	1	1	6	= 8
1727	53	27	1	= 81	6	27	4	= 37	0	1	4	= 5

Table 5. VOTES CAST IN THE EIGHTEENTH MOST POPULOUS PLACES IN THE COUNTY IN 1722, 1727 AND 1734 (MAP A)

	Population in 1801	CAESAR			SEBRIGHT			FREEMAN		PLUMER
		1722	1727	1734	1722	1727	1734	1722	1727	1734
Baldock	1,283	15	24	33	43	45	32	53	50	39
Berkhamsted	1,690	11	39	41	61	57	62	55	18	51
Bishop's Stortford	2,305	37	60	17	36	31	68	39	38	101
Braughing	972	5	14	7	33	33	37	35	39	42
Cheshunt	3,173	37	36	27	9	19	23	8	16	40
Hatfield	2,442	7	13	11	37	40	26	38	38	29
Hemel Hempstead	2,722	24	31	10	40	40	50	31	4	57
Hertford	3,360	68	73	33	6	11	30	11	10	55
Hitchin	3,161	82	135	52	25	21	75	54	11	99
Royston	975	20	28	20	19	13	22	23	22	25
St Albans	3,872	84	129	95	105	128	124	113	58	143
Sawbridgeworth	1,687	28	48	15	50	28	50	61	37	70
Standon	1,846	25	42	28	31	21	40	45	28	58
Stanstead	861	24	21	2	11	1	24	3	1	25
Stevenage	1,254	38	75	60	50	13	16	40	5	25
Tring	2,156	2	16	23	39	37	23	38	29	16
Ware	2,950	85	118	24	32	17	78	51	27	111
Watford	3,530	44	64	24	38	40	65	48	29	63
Totals		636	966	522	665	595	845	746	452	1049

Table 6A. HOW THE CLERGY VOTES WERE DISTRIBUTED IN EACH HUNDRED IN 1722 AND 1727

	CAESAR		SEBRIGHT		FREEMAN	
	1722	1727	1722	1727	1722	1727
Odsey	1	4	8	9	8	10
Edwinstree	0	3	10	8	10	11
Braughing	3	6	10	6	8	6
Hertford	2	7	6	6	5	6
Broadwater	7	8	10	5	12	4
Hitchin	1	2	7	6	6	2
Dacorum	0	5	18	17	17	11
Cashio	2	4	7	13	6	9
Totals	16	39	76	70	72	59

Table 6B. HOW THE GENTRY VOTES WERE DISTRIBUTED IN EACH HUNDRED IN 1722 AND 1727

	CAESAR		SEBRIGHT		FREEMAN	
	1722	1727	1722	1727	1722	1727
Odsey	4	9	12	9	13	12
Edwinstree	6	14	14	8	15	9
Braughing	11	33	12	12	18	13
Hertford	25	25	6	13	9	12
Broadwater	10	18	14	12	15	9
Hitchin	5	22	9	16	11	7
Dacorum	4	11	21	30	19	16
Cashio	13	24	24	26	22	17
Totals	78	156	112	126	122	95

MAP A. THE HUNDREDS OF HERTFORDSHIRE with the eighteen most populous places (cp Table 5) and the homes of the three candidates

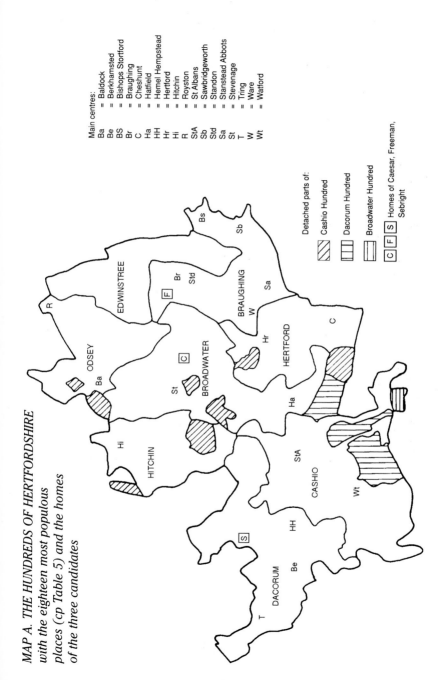

Main centres:

Ba	=	Baldock
Be	=	Berkhamsted
BS	=	Bishops Stortford
Br	=	Braughing
C	=	Cheshunt
Ha	=	Hatfield
HH	=	Hemel Hempstead
Hr	=	Hertford
Hi	=	Hitchin
R	=	Royston
StA	=	St Albans
Sb	=	Sawbridgeworth
Std	=	Standon
Sa	=	Stanstead Abbots
St	=	Stevenage
T	=	Tring
W	=	Ware
Wt	=	Watford

Detached parts of:

⍁ Cashio Hundred

⍁ Dacorum Hundred

⍁ Broadwater Hundred

C F S Homes of Caesar, Freeman, Sebright

MAP B. VOTING CHANGES BETWEEN
1722 AND 1727

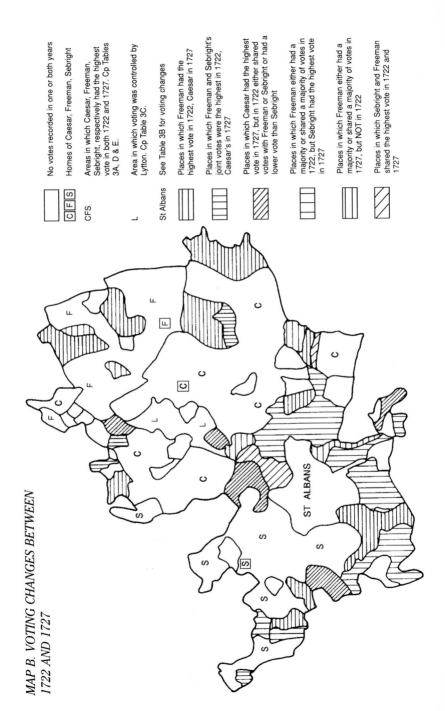

No votes recorded in one or both years

Homes of Caesar, Freeman, Sebright

Areas in which Caesar, Freeman, Sebright, respectively had the highest vote in both 1722 and 1727. Cp Tables 3A, D & E.

Area in which voting was controlled by Lytton. Cp Table 3C.

See Table 3B for voting changes

Places in which Freeman had the highest vote in 1722, Caesar in 1727

Places in which Freeman and Sebright's joint votes were the highest in 1722, Caesar's in 1727

Places in which Caesar had the highest vote in 1727, but in 1722 either shared votes with Freeman or Sebright or had a lower vote than Sebright

Places in which Freeman either had a majority or shared a majority of votes in 1722, but Sebright had the highest vote in 1727

Places in which Freeman either had a majority or shared a majority of votes in 1727, but NOT in 1722

Places in which Sebright and Freeman shared the highest vote in 1722 and 1727

PART FOUR

THE DIMSDALE FAMILY
1600-1800

TRUE QUAKERS?
THE DIMSDALE FAMILY AND THE RISE
OF THE MEDICAL PROFESSION 1600-1800

Henry Gray, as long ago as 1964, showed the fascinating link between family and occupational history. In his studies of 'Families and Trades' in Hatfield the Walby butchers stand out. He traced them from sixteenth century Watton into the twentieth century, in many Hertfordshire parishes and outside the county. Since he wrote, Walby butchers have turned up in other places in Hertfordshire.[1] Historians are familiar with the mutual self-help of Quakers and with the importance of Quaker 'dynasties' in the history of banking and chocolate, for example. The story of how one Hertfordshire family, the Dimsdales, followed the medical profession for five generations illustrates these themes. They rose with the rise of their chosen occupation and helped one another. Between the 1630s and 1780s no fewer than fourteen related Dimsdales were medical men. Seven of the fourteen were practising Quakers, others may well have been. The descendants of Robert Dimsdale, barber-alehouse keeper of Hoddesdon, include one baronet, one knight, and three MPs, two of whom were barons of the Russian Empire.

The Medical Profession
In the early seventeenth century there were three distinct groups of people who might be said to be medical men. At the top of the hierarchy were the relatively few university trained physicians. The College of Physicians was granted a charter in 1518. In 1552 it was enacted that only persons with learning and who had studied deeply might practice as physicians. As late as 1847 one member of the College gave evidence to the Select Committee on Medical Registration that society benefitted from the medical profession containing a group who had been educated with the gentry.

Way below the physicians were the surgeons. Surgery was a craft, not a profession; surgeons were apprenticed; they did not take university degrees. The gap between physicians and surgeons may have existed because of the divorce between book-learning and experience in medieval thinking and because of the church's ban on blood-shedding by priests. All university graduates were ordained. As early as 1353 surgeons acquired their own 'mystery', but in the sixteenth century they shared in the general decline in prestige of craft guilds; so in 1540 the Surgeons' and the Barbers' Guilds were united. The surgeons only separated from the barbers in 1745! The College of Physicians enforced their superior status. An Order in Council of

THE DIMSDALE FAMILY

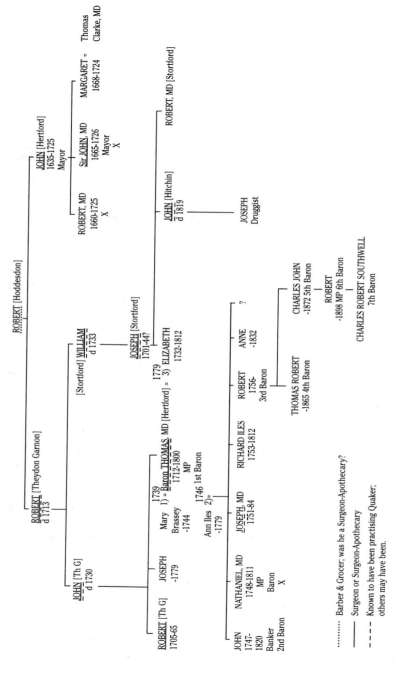

.... Barber & Grocer; was he a Surgeon-Apothecary?

——— Surgeon or Surgeon-Apothecary

– – – Known to have been practising Quaker;
others may have been.

1632 made this quite clear: it forbade surgeons undertaking any major operation such as trepanning, cutting for the stone, or opening the chest or belly, without a physician being present. As hospital provision developed, from the late sixteenth century but particularly in the eighteenth century, surgeons acquired greater expertise and began to transmit their skills through clinical teaching. In 1800 the Royal College of Surgeons received a charter.

Since physicians were few in number and surgeons increasingly tied to hospitals, the bulk of ordinary people had to rely on family receipts and village wise women. The gap left was increasingly filled by apothecaries who began as drug salesmen, the retail pharmacists of their age; they were members of the Grocers' Guild, formed in 1345. In 1542 the College of Physicians, to strengthen their hand against the surgeons, gave apothecaries the right to prescribe medicines. In 1617/18 the apothecaries separated from the Grocers' Guild, getting a charter of their own. Their right to give medical advice was reinforced by a 1703 decision.

The modern medical profession emerged as individuals crossed over from one group to another, combining different qualifications into new professional categories. Apothecaries trained as surgeons and surgeons took university degrees, qualifying as physicians. In 1815 surgeon apothecaries obtained an Act of Parliament suppressing unqualified practice and establishing a standard of regular medical education by apprenticeship and examination. A pamphleteer in 1845 wrote of the surgeon-apothecary as the general practitioner of the day, so-called because he practised all aspects of medicine, medical or surgical.

The Dimsdale family were pioneers in this process of change in the medical profession. Dimsdales appear in Hertfordshire parish registers and Quarter Sessions records in the late sixteenth and early seventeenth centuries. For example a John Demsdael, son of John Demsdael, was buried at Waltham Holy Cross in November 1565 and Robert Dimsdale, a husbandman, was buried at All Saints, Hertford in 1573; Peter Dimsdale, husbandman of Broxbourne, was presented for assault in 1624; and William Dimsdale was surveyor of highways in Cheshunt in 1638.[2] The first Dimsdale clearly identified as ancestor of all the doctors was Robert of Broxbourne and Hoddesdon. He is particularly interesting because of the evidence of the trades which he followed. In 1629 he was described as a barber of Broxbourne and presented for keeping an unlicensed alehouse. In 1630 he was presented, and compounded, for following a trade to which he had not been apprenticed for the legal seven years; the trade was grocery. In 1631 he bought the Dolphin, next to the Bull, in Hoddesdon.[3] If this is all we knew Robert might appear to have been a not uncommon example of an alehouse- or inn-keeper trying to combine several trades. However Robert's two sons were both surgeons and one was described as physician and surgeon, which arouses at least a suspicion that Robert the barber-grocer was in fact a pioneer, a would be surgeon-apothecary.

The Theydon Garnon and Bishops Stortford Dimsdales

Robert's son and namesake lived at different times at Theydon Garnon in Essex and at Bishops Stortford, in both of which places he founded medical practices. He was the first known Quaker in the family; described as a yeoman of Bishops Stortford, he was, in 1661, indicted for not attending church and committed to gaol for contempt of court. Besse records that he was released a year later in July 1662 but, in 1663, 'for practising physic without the bishop's licence Robert was excommunicated and sent to prison where he lay several years'. 'Without the bishop's licence' because, since an Act of Parliament passed in 1511, physicians and surgeons had required such a licence to practice. Besse states that Robert 'still continued prisoner on a Writ *de Excommunicato capiendo*' in 1672.[4] His persecution was not unique: there were many attacks on Hertfordshire Quakers in these years. Robert survived persecution and began to take an interest in New England where Quakers were looking for a refuge from persecution. In 1677 he bought 500 acres in West New Jersey, and in 1682 5,000 acres in Pennsylvania from William Penn for £25. He moved to New Jersey between 1683 and 1684 and took up public office there. In 1688 he began selling some of his American property and returned to Bishops Stortford. In a 1699 list of copyholders and freeholders having estates worth £10 pa, Robert Dimsdale, Quaker, appears in Bishops Stortford and Mr Robert Dimsdale in Hoddesdon. After the death of his wife in 1705 Robert returned to America and remarried there in 1713, bringing his new wife back to Bishops Stortford where he died, on 25 October 1713, and was buried in the Friends' Burial Ground.[5]

In 1663 Robert Dimsdale had been described as a surgeon but accused of 'practising physic'. In New Jersey the public records describe him as physician and surgeon. In 1684 he published *Robert Dimsdale's Advice: How to use his medicines...*, of which no copies appear to survive. So Robert appears to have followed his father's initiative in combining what were still two separate branches of medicine. He founded two long lasting medical practices, which his two sons took over. They both, incidentally, held real estate in America. John, the elder son, took over the Theydon Garnon practice; William, the younger, the Bishops Stortford one. Both brothers were Quakers and they married two Quaker sisters. Both were surgeons.[6] William's practice passed to his son Joseph, surgeon and Quaker; and from him to a son Robert who had risen professionally, acquiring a university degree. It may not be entirely a coincidence that Robert left the Society of Friends in 1764. 'Samuel Scott junior reports that himself and John Pickering have this day inquired of Robert Dimsdale of Stortford, whether he esteems himself a Member of our Society; and that the said Robert Dimsdale thereupon answered in the Negative; and that the National Worship being most agreeable to his liking as he attended the same, whereupon this Meeting esteems him no longer a Member thereto appertaining'.[7] Robert's sister, Elizabeth, married her first cousin once removed, the famous Thomas. A brother, John, moved to Hitchin. He was listed in the Militia Returns between 1765 and 1785 and in Barfoot and Wilkes 1794 directory as a surgeon; he seems to have been a surgeon-apothecary without a degree. He and his wife moved to Hertford where they died and were buried in the Friends' burial ground. John had a son Joseph, a wholesale druggist who became a partner in the firm Hankey, Williams and Dimsdale. One of his descendants was Lord Mayor of London in 1901.

To return to the elder brother, John, who died in 1730. His wife long survived her husband; she moved to Hertford and, as a member of the Friends' Meeting there, consented to her son Robert's marriage in 1737. She subscribed to Besse's *Sufferings* in 1746. This Robert took over the Theydon Garnon practice until his death in 1765. He had no heir, but the practice had continued in the family's hands from some time before the 1680s until 1765. Robert's younger brother, Thomas, became famous; before describing his career it is simplest to return to the other branch of the first Robert Dimsdale's family.

The Hertford Dimsdales

The second son of Robert Dimsdale the Broxbourne-Hoddesdon barber-grocer-alehouse keeper, John, became a major figure in the political life of Hertford Borough at the end of the seventeenth century. He was mayor in 1697-1700 and the active mover in undermining the Cowper-Whig political influence in the town (see pp 81). John and both his sons, Robert the elder and John the younger, appeared as medical witnesses in Spencer Cowper's trial. All three of them had taken part in the medical examination of Sarah Stout's body after its exhumation. The exhumation report of 1699 was signed, among others, by John Dimsdale senior, Robert Dimsdale M.D., and John Dimsdale junior. So at this date Robert the elder son had acquired the envied status of a physician; but his younger brother, John, and his father were still plain surgeons. The 1699 list of those with estates over £10 pa contains John Dimsdale of Hertford, with property in Hoddesdon and Dr Dimsdale in Little Berkhamsted.[8] In 1691 a John Dimsdale of Hertford, surgeon, had been given an order on the Standon Overseers of the Poor 'for the cure of one Philip Hughs his thigh which was broken by a waggon within the said parish'.[9] This was probably the father. Robert, gentleman of All Saints Hertford, was not always as well behaved as might have been expected of the first graduate in the family. In 1696 he was indicted for assaulting Leonard Dell the Hertford bellman, by throwing cold water on his head in the Salutation alehouse.[10] This can hardly have been a medical student's prank for Robert was thirty-six.

The three Dimsdales were active in Hertford Borough politics into the 1720s, voting for the Tories, in particular consistently supporting Charles Caesar. In the general election of July 1702, for example, Mr Justice Dimsdale, Dr Robert and John Dimsdale junior all voted the Tory ticket. In 1706 one of the John Dimsdales was mayor and in 1708 a John Dimsdale was à parliamentary candidate but defeated. In 1711 John Dimsdale was mayor again and in 1722 again stood, unsuccessfully, for parliament. The younger John qualified as a physician and was knighted. His sister, Margaret, married another M.D., Thomas Clarke. None of these Hertford Dimsdales, apparently, were Quakers. It may be, however, that having Quaker cousins made it easier for them to form the long lasting political alliance first created in 1699 between Hertford Tories and the local Quakers. The elder John and Robert both died in 1725, Sir John in 1726. The two brothers were buried in All Saints, Hertford where memorials described Robert as 'a learned and skilled physician' and Sir John, in significantly different language, as 'a good physician and so eminent a Surgeon that he left behind him few equals, none superior in that profession'.[11] Lady Susan, Sir John's widow, survived him for many years. This rich lady, with powerful local connections, probably played an important part in the early career of Thomas Dimsdale, younger son of John of Theydon Garnon.

Thomas, Baron Dimsdale and his family

Thomas Dimsdale was born in 1712, apprenticed as a surgeon to his father, John, in Theydon Garnon and then studied at St Thomas' hospital in London.[12] It was William Cheselden of St Thomas' who first lectured on anatomy, in 1711. In effect Thomas had about as complete a surgical education as was available in his day. In 1734 he set up in practice on his own in Hertford where Dimsdales had practised for some fifty years but not for the previous eight years. This connection, which the widowed Lady Susan Dimsdale symbolised, must have helped Thomas establish himself. In addition he was a birthright Friend, properly introduced to the Hertford Meeting, with a certificate of clearness in respect of marriage engagements, by his previous Meeting, Enfield. The Quakers, though no longer so many or so influential as they had been forty years earlier, still carried much weight in the town. Five years after reaching Hertford Thomas married; his wife, Mary, was the daughter of Nathaniel Brassey who was

MP for Hertford Borough from 1734 to 1761. The Brasseys were not Quakers and marriage outside the Society was forbidden to Quakers. Thomas' marriage may have made him more acceptable in local society and advanced his practice, but it did him no good with the local Friends' Meeting. The detailed record of what took place, as recorded in the local Minute Book, is worth quoting in full. It is a revealing indication of the extraordinary combination of doctrinaire rigidity and patient persistence which marked eighteenth century Quakers. At the same time it reveals Thomas Dimsdale as apparently anxious to preserve his Quaker connection:

'6.6.1739. Ralph Thorn acquainted this Meeting, that he did not ask Thomas Dimsdale for his Collection, on account of his having Married a Person not of our Society; this Meeting therefore desires him not to Ask him for it, till such time as he shall have given Satisfaction for his said Offence; for which End the Meeting appoints

Plate 10
Thomas
Baron Dimsdale
(1712-1800)
[British Museum].

John Pryor and Thomas Grubb to Treat with him thereupon, and endeavour to make him Sensible thereof.'

'3.7.1739. John Pryor and Thomas Grubb report they have Visited Thomas Dimsdale and tho' he gave them a full Oppertunity of Treating with him yet he did not seem at present Disposed to clear the Truth from the Reproach he has brought upon it the further Treating with him is continued to the said Friends when Oppertunity may be suitable.'

Such entries continue regularly until the climax:

'29.7.1740.... the Labour of Love bestowed upon him by this Meeting hath had such Effect as to occasion his Sending by them a Paper to this Meeting, wherein he acknowledges that the Circumstances of his Marriage have tended to the Disreputation of the Society, and sincerely desires that his Offence may be passed by. The consideration ...deferred.'

'3.9.1740.... the said Paper is not sufficient to clear the Truth and the Society from that Reproach which his Marriage and the Circumstances attending it have brought upon them, and therefore desires the Friends before appointed to Visit him again.'

Visits continued and a testimony against Thomas Dimsdale and his action was drawn up in July 1741:

'28.10.1741. Read over, and maturely considered, is Agreed to:... Whereas Thomas Dimsdale of Hertford hath Joyned in marriage with a person not of our Religious Society, and in such a Way and manner as is contrary to the Good Order and Discipline established amongst Friends; for which he hath been repeatedly Treated with by this meeting that he might be brought to a true Sense of his Disorderly practice and from thence might give this Meeting due Satisfaction for his said Offence; but finding no hopes thereof and having waited upon him a long Time This Meeting therefore, for the Clearing of the holy Truth and Friends, doth hereby Testify against the said Thomas Dimsdale... and declare that We cannot have Unity with him as a Member of our Religious Society, untill he comes to a sincere Sorrow for his said offence, and by his acknowledgement thereof, and future Walking agreeable to our holy profession, he render himself fitt to be again Received into Unity with Friends which is what We do heartily desire for him. Which Testimony the Clerk is desired to deliver Thomas Dimsdale a true Copy of.'

On 1 January 1742 the Clerk reported to the Hertford Meeting that he had delivered this testimony to Thomas Dimsdale and on 29 January it was reported that it had been read to a Meeting for Worship in Hertford again.[13] The extraordinary fact is that, in spite of this uncharitable treatment, Thomas Dimsdale apparently remained a Friend. Whether he continued to attend the Meeting in spite of being disowned or resumed attendance after his wife's death in 1744 we do not know. In 1768 he spoke of the Quakers, to Catherine the Great, as though he was a practising Friend. In 1775 his son, Joseph, was admitted to membership since he 'has been brought up from the Early part of his Time to attend our Meetings for Worship, and having persevered in the same commendable line of conduct'.[14] When he died in 1800 Thomas was buried in the Friends Burial Ground at Bishops Stortford with his second and third wives. In his draft will of 1790 he left £10 for the Stortford Meeting House and the burial register does not record him as a non-member.[15] Probably at some time or other he was re-admitted to membership by the Friends.

When his first wife, Mary, died in 1744 Thomas left Hertford and joined the Duke of Cumberland's army fighting Prince Charles Edward, as an unpaid surgeon. In 1746 he was back in Hertford and married again, to Ann Iles, a relative of his first wife who brought him some estate and produced ten children for him, eight of whom were boys. About this time Lady Susan Dimsdale left him a considerable fortune. He moved into the Priory and ceased to practice but he could not give up medicine for ever. In 1761 he took his MD at Aberdeen University; he was forty-nine. He began to specialise in the treatment of smallpox and became outstanding as an inoculator. This inoculation treatment, by infecting a patient with smallpox, preceded vaccination with cowpox by many years. Among Thomas' early patients were John Scott, the Quaker poet of Amwell, and his fellow Quaker, Joseph Cockfield. They became Thomas' patients in April 1766. Cockfield wrote on 15 April 1766: 'I set out for Hertfordshire tomorrow, in order to be inoculated by Dr Dimsdale. I hope however, if the disease proves favourable, to return in a fortnight. . The Doctor has at present amazing success with persons of all constitutions and degrees.'[16]

In 1767 Thomas Dimsdale published the first of several treatises, *The Present Method of Inoculating for the Smallpox*. It went into six editions in five years and was translated into several European languages. Dimsdale's skill became famous and, in 1768, he was invited to Russia to inoculate Catherine the Great and her son, the future Czar Paul. Thomas and his son, Nathaniel, then a medical student at Edinburgh university who accompanied and assisted his father, were lavishly rewarded by the royal family and Russian nobility. Both father and son were made Barons of the Russian Empire. On their return to England Thomas was made a Fellow of the Royal Society; this was in 1769. Back in Hertford, Thomas continued inoculating the famous and ordinary people alike. In 1774 that reluctant 'noble savage' from Otahiti, Omiah, was sent to Thomas Dimsdale for inoculation. As well as the house of reception, a nursing home for such patients before and after inoculation, Dimsdale opened an 'inoculating house' for poor patients. In 1781 he returned to Russia to inoculate younger members of the royal family. This time his third wife, Elizabeth, his first cousin once removed, accompanied him. There were more rewards.

Thomas Dimsdale's Russian triumph changed his life style. By 1769 the bank of Dimsdale, Archer and Byde was in existence; in 1775 another Dimsdale joined the bank. Thomas' sons were established in banking. When Gurney's bank was opened in 1775 they employed a manager trained in the Dimsdale bank in Cornhill. In 1780 Thomas was elected MP for Hertford Borough; he was re-elected in 1784. He must have ceased regular practice about this time though he went to Russia in 1781 and in 1786 his old friend, Samuel Scott wrote: 'Yesterday I had a conference with my worthy friend the baron, concerning the use of sea-water which he rather recommended' for Scott's bad legs. In 1787 Scott wrote: 'I was seized near the Castle with a suspension of Strength that I seemed both to myself and those who accidentally passed by in the Agonies of Death... The baron thought it not safe to come to London for some days.'[17] Dimsdale was losing his sight until Wenzel performed a remarkable cataract operation in 1783. In 1790 the baron did not stand for re-election. His place as MP for Hertford Borough was taken by his second son, Nathaniel, by this time a graduate physician practising in London. In their last years Thomas and his wife, Elizabeth, passed their winters in Bath. Thomas died in 1800, aged eighty-eight.

John the banker, Thomas' eldest son, inherited the title. He had no children and the title passed to Robert, the fifth son, whose son, Thomas Robert, became the fourth baron. He died in 1865 without male heirs, at Essendon, where he had bought property in 1832. There were three brothers, two of them graduate doctors, between John and Robert. None of them left male heirs. Nathaniel, a baron in his own right, was buried in 1811 in Hertford as an Anglican. Joseph died in 1784; he was a Quaker. Richard Iles died in 1812. When Thomas Robert died in 1865 the title passed to Charles John Dimsdale, his brother, who also lived in Essendon, but not in the same house as his elder brother. He assembled an estate around Scales Park wood then in the parish of Barkway, now in Nuthampstead, which also included land in Meesden. Scales Park had been bought by his grandfather Thomas in the 1750s. Charles John died in 1872 and was succeeded by his son, Robert, the sixth baron who became MP for Hertford Borough 1866-74 and for the Hitchin Division 1885-92. He died in 1898 and was succeeded by his son, Charles Robert Southwell Dimsdale, the seventh baron, who completed a house at Meesden and moved into it in 1906, selling Essendon Place in 1912. The family later moved to Barkway where they still live. The Dimsdale bank survived to the end of the nineteenth century and there was at least one Dimsdale practising medicine in the middle of the twentieth century.[18] In five generations the Dimsdales had risen from aspiring tradesmen to become established as a county family, respected sufficiently to become local MPs. They began as surgeons and by the turn of the eighteenth-nineteenth centuries the family contained physicians, two of whom had foreign titles, while others were bankers.

NOTES

1   Henry Gray *Hatfield and its People* Book 11A pp 30-33. Lionel M Munby (edit) *Wheathampstead and Harpenden IV The Age of Independence* pp 169-70. Walby butchers appear in the Hitchin militia lists for example.

2   *Hertfordshire County Records. Calendar to the Sessions Books* Vol V 1619-57, pp 32 and 266.

3   *Ibid.* pp 132, 131; Vol III, p 252; and HCRO. D1068/9. C M Matthews, in *Haileybury since Roman Times* (1959), Chap XIII, describes Robert and his descendants' lives.

4   *Ibid.* Vol VI 1658-1700, pp 47 & 50; Joseph Besse *A Collection of the Sufferings of the People called Quakers.* London (1753), Vol 1, pp 244 & 250.

5   Milton Rubincam 'Dr Robert Dimsdale: pioneer physician and colonial legislator' in *Proceedings of the New Jersey Historical Society* Vol 57, No 2 (April 1939) pp 98-107; and Sessions Books *op. cit.* Vol II, pp 7 & 15.

6   Violet Rowe in her history of *The First Hertford Quakers* writes of a young William Dimsdale who in the early 1670s became an Independent, claiming to have been a Quaker but to have broken with them. 'His parents were not Friends, and when they discovered that Thomas Grigson, a Hertford weaver to whom they had apprenticed their son, was a Quaker' they took steps to ensure he attended a church service (p.31). This cannot have been William the surgeon.

7   Minutes of the Friends' Meeting for 24 September 1764. HCRO. Q87.

8   Sessions Books *op. cit.* Vol II, pp 15 & 21.

9   *Ibid.* Vol VI, p438.

10   *Ibid.* Vol I, pp 424-5.

11   Lewis Turnor *History of the Ancient Town and Borough of*

Hertford. pp 202 & 210.

12 Accounts of Thomas Dimsdale's life can be found in the *DNB;* in the *Gentleman's Magazine* of July 1801, reprinted in VCH. Herts, *Genealogical Volume* p 9; and in Turnor *op. cit.* pp 166-8. Fuller accounts of the baron's and his son's visits to Russia and of his inoculation techniques are in I M Graham 'Two Hertfordshire Doctors' in *East Herts Archaeological Society Transactions* Vol XIII, Part 1 1950-51, pp 44 & 46-54; in W J Bishop 'Thomas Dimsdale, MD, FRS (1712-1800) and the inoculation of Catherine the Great of Russia' in *Annals of Medical History* Vol IV, No 4 July 1932, pp 321-338 which has a bibliography; and in Philip H Clendenning 'Dr Thomas Dimsdale and Smallpox Inoculation in Russia' in *Journal of the History of Medicine and Allied Sciences* Vol XXVIII, No 2 April 1973.

13 HCRO Q85 & Q86.

14 HCRO Q88 – 4 and 25 December 1775.

15 HCRO D/EL F 10

16 Lawrence D Stewart *John Scott of Amwell.* p 39.

17 Letters to John Dimsdale of Hitchin in Dimsdale Mss. Folder 1, 16 & 18, Friends Meeting House.

18 *VCH. Herts. Genealogical Volume* (1907), p 9; Vol 3 (1912), pp 429, 458-9 & 461; Vol 4 (1914), pp 88 & 90; Turnor *op. cit.* pp 257-8; and information from Robert Dimsdale esq. of Barkway, to whose generosity I owe much other information, several references, the sight of family papers, and loan of several of the publications quoted.

INDEX